THE SEEKER'S GUIDE TO

Mary

D1173358

Other books in the Seeker Series include

Living the Beatitudes Today
Bill Dodds and Michael J. Dodds, O.P.

The Seeker's Guide to Being Catholic
Mitch Finley

The Seeker's Guide to Building a Christian Marriage
Kathleen Finley

The Seeker's Guide to Jesus in the Gospels
Steve Mueller

The Seeker's Guide to Reading the Bible
Steve Mueller

The Seeker's Guide to Saints
Mitch Finley

The Seeker's Guide to 7 Life-Changing Virtues
Bill Dodds and Michael J. Dodds, O.P.

The Seeker's Guide to the Christian Story
Mitch Finley

The Seeker's Guide to the Rosary
Liz Kelly

Chicago

THE SEEKER'S GUIDE TO
Mary

LOYOLAPRESS.

CHICAGO

MARÍA RUIZ SCAPERLANDA

LOYOLAPRESS.

3441 N. ASHLAND AVENUE
CHICAGO, ILLINOIS 60657

© 2002 by María Ruiz Scaperlanda
All rights reserved

The Seeker Series from Loyola Press provides trustworthy guides for your journey of faith. It is dedicated to the principle that asking questions is not only all right, but essential.

Scripture extracts are taken from the *New American Bible,* copyright © 1970 by the Confraternity of Christian Doctrine, Inc., Washington, D.C. Used with permission. All rights reserved. No part of the *New American Bible* may be reproduced by any means without permission in writing from the copyright owner.

"The Incarnation" (p. xxvi) is from *The Collected Works of St. John of the Cross,* translated by Kieran Kavanaugh and Otilio Rodriguez, copyright © 1979, 1991 by the Washington Province of Discalced Carmelites, Inc., ICS Publications, 2131 Lincoln Road, N.E., Washington, D.C., 20002-1199, U.S.A. Used with permission.

Credits continued on page 219

Cover template and interior design by Lisa Buckley
Cover image: Scala/Art Resource, NY

Library of Congress Cataloging-in-Publication Data
Scaperlanda, María Ruiz, 1960–
   The seeker's guide to Mary / María Ruiz Scaperlanda.
     p. cm.
   Includes bibliographical references.
   ISBN 0-8294-1489-4
    1. Mary, Blessed Virgin, Saint. I. Title.

 BT603 .S32 2002
 232.91—dc21   2001038646

Printed in Canada

02 03 04 05 06 07 08 09 Webcom 9 8 7 6 5 4 3 2 1

For my mom, María de Jesús,
herself named after Jesus' mother,
who taught me to recognize Mary
as my mother in heaven

Contents

Acknowledgments

I owe first thanks to Jim Manney of Loyola Press for inviting me to write this book—and for his persistent patience with my process. Your guidance, vision, encouragement, and confidence in me have been a source of grace and a wonderful blessing.

Thanks to my parents, Ignacio and María de Jesús, especially Mom, to whom this book is dedicated. Thank you for sharing with me over the years your intimate relationship with *la virgencita.*

And special thanks to my husband, Michael, my fellow seeker and soul mate, and to my awesome foursome—Christopher, Anamaría, Rebekah, and Michelle—who make it a point to encourage me in my writing and who demand that I maintain a sense of humor!

Finally, thanks to the staff and editors of Loyola Press, who have made working on every step of this project such a wonderful experience.

A Word to the Seeker:
There's Something about Mary

Virgin mother, daughter of thy son, lowly and
*   uplifted more than any creature, fixed goal of*
*   the eternal counsel,*
thou art she who didst human nature so ennoble
*   that its own Maker scorned not to become*
*   its making.*
In thy womb was lit again the love under whose
*   warmth in the eternal peace this flower hath*
*   thus unfolded.*
Here art thou unto us the meridian torch of
*   love and there below with mortals art a*
*   living spring of hope.*
Lady thou art so great and hast such worth,
*   that if there be who would have grace yet*
*   betaketh not himself to thee, his longing*

seeketh to fly without wings.

Thy kindliness not only succoureth whoso re-
questeth, but doth oftentimes freely forerun
request.

In thee is tenderness, in thee is pity, in thee
munificence, in thee united whatever in created
being is of excellence.

ST. BERNARD'S PRAYER TO THE VIRGIN MARY
From Dante's *Divine Comedy,* Canto XXXIII

Not long ago, Mary made the cover of *Time* magazine, the eighth time to date that she has turned up within the famous red border. She has been the subject of numerous cinematic projects, including the recent made-for-TV movie *Mary, the Mother of Jesus.* Modern artists love to either attack or embrace her as the eminent icon of femininity. Popular novelists at times present her as a dark-skinned Aztec woman in order to have her embody a sense of Hispanic culture or ethnicity. And paralleling our widespread interest in angels, miracles, and the afterlife, new books on Mary continue the decades-long trend of publications on the religious and spiritual significance of this young woman from Nazareth.

In the Catholic Church today, Mary is frequently presented as an example of piety, trust, and obedience, a faithful woman whose actions are heralded by some as unique manifestations of radical feminism. A strong and free woman, Mary is active, courageous, and intelligent, an example of a good woman who attests to a feminine capacity for grace and glory. At times, she is introduced as a representation of the feminine power of God. And although Mary is said to be a point of division between Catholics and Protestants, she remains central to the beliefs of all Christians. Without Mary, there can be no Bethlehem story.

The varied perspectives of Mary can make learning about her a challenge. Yet there are many sources we can consult in order to develop an understanding of this woman of remarkable faith. This book offers an introduction to Mary by discussing what we know of her through Scripture and history as well as what we have come to believe about her through centuries of tradition and faith.

Mary of Nazareth has hardly been a uniform figure across history, languages, and cultures, but her constant presence is undeniable in the lives of the faithful, regardless of historical or cultural differences. Marian devotion has taken on many forms and has developed many traditions within specific cultures, such as special prayers, cultural representations of Mary, and artistic interpretations of scriptural stories about her. The representations of the mother of Jesus are complex and varied, but the central reason why Mary is so embedded in our cultural traditions is quite simple: Mary is a key figure in the divine story of our salvation. Yet Mary was a woman. She was a daughter, a wife, a mother. We can relate to Mary's human joy, her suffering, and her hope. We can understand how difficult it must have been for an unwed and suddenly pregnant young woman to trust in God's plan for her life. We can feel Mary's awe as the child grew within her, and we can feel her joy at giving birth to new life. We can imagine her sense of hope as she taught Jesus and watched her baby grow into a young man. We can also suffer the brokenness and extreme agony she suffered as she watched her own Son suffer and, ultimately, held his dead body in her arms. We can relate to Mary in a personal way because she walked a very human journey.

Who Is Mary, Really?

When I was a young child growing up on the southern shores of Puerto Rico, I attended a Catholic school named Academia Santa María in the developing industrial town of Ponce. Although I lived in Ponce for only a couple of years, I have fond memories of that time, especially as the period when I was first introduced to devotional prayers in an academic setting. It was at Santa María that I first said a rosary with my classmates. I remember vividly how hard it was for me as a kindergartner to sit through Mass every week and how I became a member of the school club called las Bernarditas, named after St. Bernadette of Lourdes. Since my full name (or as I call it, my real name) is María de Lourdes—in English, Mary of Lourdes—I was especially taken by the fact that so many "big" girls wanted to be in this club. I was impressed that these older girls found it important to ask Mary for her protection and intercession on behalf of each of us as "women." I still have, in a keepsake box, the small ribbon and medal of St. Bernadette that I received upon entering the club.

As I've grown older, Mary has remained a part of my life, even if I have not always been attuned to her presence. She was the topic of some of my first poems as a child, the kind of poems written by flashlight in a notebook kept hidden underneath the bed. It was Mary to whom I cried for comfort when I was a new kid in a strange school, with all the inhibitions and fears that such a situation naturally brings. I don't know why or how my devotion to Mary started. It somehow just seemed natural to talk to Mary, a mother, when it appeared that no one else could possibly understand how I felt. Years later, when I became a mother myself, I instinctively turned to Mary with my fears, hopes, and dreams for my own children.

These are not theological or philosophical reasons for the religious importance of Mary, but I suspect they are not an unusual starting place for a Christian who tries to understand Jesus and his life through Scripture and to then make the connection between that understanding and his or her own life experience. We speak of Mary with special respect for two critical reasons, both of which are Scripture based.

First, Mary is the mother of Jesus, the Son of God. As such, Mary was an essential part of God's plan of salvation.

Our understanding of Mary is rooted in Scripture and grows out of two thousand years of devotion, piety, and theological reflection. Church tradition teaches that Mary was preserved from original sin in view of God calling her to be the mother of Jesus. She was gifted in grace beyond measure and fulfilled her role in a unique pilgrimage of faith, thus becoming the mother of the church and the spiritual mother of all people.

We call Mary "mother," a symbolic title given to her by Jesus at Calvary on behalf of the body of believers, as represented by the beloved disciple:

> Near the cross of Jesus there stood his mother, his mother's sister, Mary the wife of Clopas, and Mary Magdalene. Seeing his mother there with the disciple whom he loved, Jesus said to his mother, "Woman, there is your son." In turn he said to the disciple, "There is your mother." From that hour onward, the disciple took her into his care. (John 19:25–27)

In a later chapter, we will further discuss the central understanding of Mary as the mother of God, *Theotokos,* ("God-bearer")—one of the greatest paradoxes in the Christian faith. Understood definitively by the early Christians since the Council of Ephesus in 431, this title calls for the church to honor Mary with special reverence because, as the most holy mother of God, she was, after her Son, exalted above all angels and people. In Mary's own prophetic

A WORD TO THE SEEKER

words, "all ages to come shall call me blessed. / God who is mighty has done great things for me" (Luke 1:48–49).

Jesus Christ is the one sent by God to mediate between God and humankind. To assert this truth, however, does not preclude our acknowledging Mary's mediating role. The term *mediatrix* from the Latin word *medius,* meaning "in the middle," was first used with regard to Mary in the eighth century. Like a human mother advocating on behalf of her children, she mediates on our behalf when we ask her to offer our humble petitions and prayers to God. We recognize that Mary's part in the story of salvation is entirely subordinate to that of Christ. We also remain aware that, from the outset, Mary was an agent of mediation because she freely cooperated with God by responding, "Let it be done to me as you say" (Luke 1:38) at the archangel Gabriel's news of the Incarnation. We believe that, even now, Mary cooperates in extending Christ's grace to us by her maternal intercession from heaven on our behalf.

A second reason for addressing Mary with special respect is that she was the first disciple of Jesus, the first to "hear the word of God and act upon it" (Luke 8:21). Mary was the first one to acknowledge and believe the truth proclaimed by the messenger of God, that "the holy offspring to be born will be called Son of God" (Luke 1:35). In an authentic way, Mary was the first Christian, the first to choose to follow her people's Messiah. She was the first to believe in and to be confused by the way in which her Son's life was unfolding. She was the first, at the foot of the cross, to acknowledge the mystery of what was happening. The Son she gave birth to—the Son of God, the Messiah, the Prince of Peace—was a contradiction to the world as he lived out God's plan of salvation all the way to his violent death.

Because she is human, Mary is one with all human beings in our need for salvation. Yet by her unique cooperation with God's plan of salvation, she also became for each of us a model of what it means to say yes to God in our individual lives. Mary is the first—and the ultimate—example of discipleship. For these reasons, the church, the body of believers, honors her with affection and devotion. In the words of noted poet and author Kathleen Norris, from her book *Amazing Grace:*

> I treasure Mary as a biblical interpreter, one who heard and believed what God told her, and who pondered God's promise in her heart, even when, as the Gospel of Luke describes it, it pierced her soul like a sword. This is . . . the kind of faith that sustains Christian discipleship. Mary's life is as powerful an evocation of what it can mean to be God's chosen as the life of Moses, or St. Paul. (118)

We call Mary "blessed" because of her unequivocal faith and surrender to God. In the first chapter of Luke, the angel Gabriel calls Mary of Nazareth the "highly favored daughter" of God, adding, "The Lord is with you. Blessed are you among women." As we will discuss later, this honoring of Mary, the woman who "found favor with God," was a tradition from the beginning of Christianity. In the writings of the early Christians, we read of Mary, holy and free from sin, who gave her full heart to God and was declared "full of grace" by the angel Gabriel.

We honor the Blessed Virgin Mary's unique role in our salvation through our liturgy and our other prayer traditions. Marian piety has hardly disappeared, as some historians once predicted it would. The Catholic Church's revised Roman calendar celebrates fifteen Marian feasts that honor Mary's role in the birth and life of Jesus, celebrate the grace in her own life, and hail her as a model of Christian living and as an instrument of grace. In every Mass, moreover, Mary is remembered along with the apostles, martyrs, and all the saints during the eucharistic prayer and the proclamation of the Apostles' Creed. Throughout church history, private and communal prayers—the Hail Mary; the Hail, Holy Queen; the Memorare; the Angelus—have celebrated Mary's life and the unparalleled gift of her Son to each of us. And Mary continues to fascinate the imagination and challenge the faith of believers and nonbelievers alike through regular and sometimes outrageous reports of apparitions and sightings.

We can relate to Mary in a personal way because she walked a very human journey.

Mary's Singular Purpose

A woman of many names and countless forms, Mary has appeared continuously across the centuries in art, literature, and music. In visual art, Mary is often portrayed with a distinct halo, symbolizing her holiness. Many artists depict her holding the baby Jesus or looking graciously over him in his manger or straw crib. Others depict her as the Queen of Heaven, crowned by stars and with a crescent moon underfoot. Gracious and stately, she is often surrounded by angels. Her head is often draped with a veil, and she frequently holds a rosary. Sometimes her heart is pierced. And sometimes the Madonna is depicted as saints have seen her in their mystic visions.

The first artistic rendition of Mary that we know of is a third-century fresco on a wall of the underground chamber of the Catacombs of Priscilla, on the ancient Via Salaria in Rome. When I first saw this painting, known simply as the Madonna and Child, I was instantly struck by the simplicity and tenderness still evident in what's left of the plaster image. Mary is seated on a throne and is clad in a short-sleeved tunic with a *palla* covering her head. Her body is slightly inclined, in an attitude of motherly tenderness toward the child she holds in her arms. Next to her stands a prophet— some say Balaam, others Isaiah—who points with his right hand toward the star above Mary's head, no doubt a scriptural allusion that would have been obvious to early Christians visiting the burial place.

Roughly thirteen hundred years later, Leonardo da Vinci's famous painting *The Virgin of the Rocks* presented in Mary—much as his Mona Lisa presented—a notion of ideal and perfect beauty. Here a haloed Mary appears at the forefront of an elaborate rocky landscape. This young, beautiful Mary looks away from Jesus and the other characters. All of Mary's emotion resides in her expressive hands, her right hand resting tenderly on the shoulder of the infant John the Baptist while her left hand hovers protectively above the head of her Son. Mary's facial expression is blank, detached, unemotional, as if her showing some kind of feeling would somehow desecrate our perception of her. The Spanish painter Luis de Morales depicted a delicate and beautiful woman in his sixteenth-century painting *The Virgin and Child.* I love how this image breaks from the conventional representations of Mary: the baby Jesus lightheartedly plays with his mother's clothes, sticking his right hand into her bosom, a natural and intimate gesture familiar to most mothers.

Perhaps the best-known representation of Mary and Jesus is Michelangelo's *Pietà,* a remarkable sculpture depicting a sorrowful mother mourning her crucified Son. In this work, which Michelangelo created before he was thirty years old, Mary holds the lifeless Christ in her arms as his right arm with its pierced hand hangs in the limpness of death. This white marble sculpture continues to attract large crowds at St. Peter's Basilica in Rome. Thousands of visitors stand in front of this shocking depiction of death, sorrow, and pain. Without being told to keep quiet, visitors instinctively speak softly, if at all, gazing in respect at the overwhelming agony of a mother who must bury the child she bore.

My personal image and understanding of Mary were greatly influenced by the 1977 film *Jesus of Nazareth.* In this rich cinematic interpretation of the life of Jesus, Mary is again portrayed as young, virtuous, and beautiful. Italian director Franco Zeffirelli depicts a godly and devout Jewish woman as he beautifully recreates all the biblical stories traditionally associated with Mary: the Annunciation, the birth of Jesus, the visitation of the Magi, and Mary and Joseph finding Jesus in the temple.

But Zeffirelli's portrayal of Mary at the Crucifixion is like nothing I have seen in any other artistic medium. When the lifeless body of her Son is taken down from the wooden cross, this Mary drops to her knees screaming, grabs the bloodied, mangled body, and embraces it, rocking back and forth with him as she surely would have done when he was a baby. As in Michelangelo's *Pietà*, Mary clutches the limp body of her Son, his head and arms at unnatural angles beside her. But everything in this Mary's face shows the searing pain of a woman who has just lost her child. The sky cries in torrential rain as Mary, the mother of the One who came to save the world, screams out in sorrow and anguish to her God, who has asked of her such an unthinkable act of surrender.

This is a mother I can relate to. My own heart is moved and torn deep within me as I gaze upon Mary's distorted facial expression. I can conceive the heartbreak, the loss, the despair of a situation that I honestly hope and pray I will never have to live through. I can imagine no greater pain than having to hold my own child dead in my arms. Mary's heart inevitably cried to heaven in anguish even as she faithfully clung to God and continued to entrust her life and her only Son to him.

Every person, we believe, has a unique purpose in life, and this purpose becomes a singular way to image the divine. Mary's purpose was and is to be the mother of Jesus. Through Jesus, she is also the mother of his Mystical Body, the church. Yet in our human desire to understand what kind of young woman could give birth to the Son of God, we have often portrayed Mary solely as an example of utmost piety, ignoring the realities that she, like us, had to endure. When we portray Mary in this way, we do her and ourselves a disservice. It is not only what sets Mary apart from us that makes her special, but also all that she has in common with each of us as a follower of Christ, as a woman, and as a mother.

In her dignity and faithfulness, in her strength and tireless devotion to God, Mary embodies the heart of discipleship. Not exclusively a Martha or a Mary, she successfully lived out a balance between an active life and a contemplative spirit.

Mary's work as a mother and her response of ministry and mission are critical to our understanding of her. She was, no doubt, a practical, efficient, and devout laborer within her culture. But it was Mary's prayer life that gave meaning to her work and to her life. It was in quiet that Mary received the grace of wisdom. It was in prayer that she allowed the strength of God to become real in her life. These facts are not only relevant to Mary's life; they also provide a model for each person who claims to be a believer in Christ.

What Are Our Sources?

The biblical references to Mary come to life and make sense because they are part of the career and significance of Jesus and of the Evangelists' communication of God's plan of salvation. The earliest Christian preaching about Jesus concerned his death and resurrection, not his birth. In fact, biblical scholars point out that one may speak of the Gospels as developing backward. Jesus' death and resurrection, after all, provided the clearest understanding of God's salvific action, as well as a personal understanding of who Jesus was. Over time, as the oral traditions about Jesus' ministry— collections of sayings, stories of miracles, parables—grew and began to be written down, the material was arranged in a logical structure. As Scripture scholar Raymond E. Brown notes, "In such a process of Gospel formation, selection and emphasis were dictated by the fact that a message of salvation was being preached and taught," and the form became particularly useful "as further teaching for those who had come to faith through the proclamation of the death and resurrection" (*The Birth of the Messiah*, 27). The Gospel of Mark, written in the late seventh decade and considered by most scholars to be the oldest account of Jesus, has no birth narrative. "The gospel of Jesus Christ, the Son of God" (1:1) begins with the encounter of Jesus and John the Baptist at the Jordan. "In the early Christian preaching the birth of Jesus had not yet been seen in the same salvific light as the death and resurrection," says Brown, noting that there is no reference at all to Jesus' birth in the Acts of the Apostles and only one specific reference in the main Pauline letters (*Birth*, 28).

The two Gospel narratives of Jesus' birth, the Gospel stories with by far the most scriptural references to Jesus' mother, are found in Matthew and Luke, believed to have been written in the ninth decade, roughly two decades after Mark's Gospel. While "an intelligent case can be made for the historicity of the details in the infancy narratives that have a close relationship to Christian doctrine," the two birth narratives are not only different but are even contrary to each other in a number of details. In his comprehensive work *The Birth of the Messiah*, Raymond Brown argues for an understanding of the birth narratives as theology rather than as history (37). Whether or not the infancy narratives are historical, whether or not they are based on eyewitness testimony, and whether or not they had a "pre-Gospel" existence, it is "precisely because the material has been less fixed in the course of apostolic preaching [that] the evangelists exercised greater freedom of composition in the infancy narratives" (*Birth*, 38).

Given the early evangelical emphasis on Jesus' passion, death, and resurrection and the relatively few biblical references to Mary, the narrative tradition of the church during its first few hundred years provides a critical element to our knowledge and understanding of Mary of Nazareth. Since its infancy and still today, the church has contemplated the biblical references to Mary in an attempt to understand her unique role in God's plan for our salvation. What we know of Mary and what has become Marian theology through the church is based on Scripture and tradition. From the start, Mary—the character in God's story of salvation and the faithful handmaiden of the Lord—was a special means by which God reached humanity and became Love. She was an instrument of grace, allowing salvation to be born into this world.

It is also important to remember that what the church has proclaimed as doctrine about Mary was born out of a tradition that was common to all Christians. St. Ignatius of Antioch (c. 35–c. 107), in his letter to the Smyrnaeans, first used the term *catholic* in reference to the universal church. In this letter, he also assumed a body of belief common to the faithful everywhere. This body of common belief existed until the Eastern Schism (1054), after which the Eastern Church began to call itself "Orthodox."

It is not only what sets Mary apart from us that makes her special, but also all that she has in common with each of us as a follower of Christ, as a woman, and as a mother.

Introducing: Mary of Nazareth

As an introductory guide to Mary, this book is in no way a comprehensive exploration into the life of this remarkable woman. This is not a theological treatise of Marian devotion, nor is it an exhaustive presentation of the church's doctrine on Mary or her apparitions.

It is a beginning, an introduction.

Yet it is my hope and my prayer that from this beginning, Mary—the woman, the mother, the disciple—will be seen in her fullness for all that she, the very first Christian, has to offer us through her life, her faith, and her example.

Then he called
the archangel Gabriel
and sent him to
the virgin Mary,
at whose consent
the mystery was wrought,
in whom the Trinity
clothed the Word with flesh.
and though Three work this,
it is wrought in the One;
and the Word lived incarnate
in the womb of Mary.
And he who had only a Father
now had a Mother too,
but she was not like others
who conceive by man.
From her own flesh
he received his flesh,
so he is called
Son of God and of man.

—*ST. JOHN OF THE CROSS*
"The Incarnation"

CHAPTER ONE

Mary in Scripture

Marian traditions and feasts abound in the Catholic Church, but what does Scripture have to say about this most blessed of women? Mary is mentioned only nineteen times in the New Testament, most often in the Gospels of Matthew and Luke, both written no earlier than eight decades after the events they describe. To a large extent, Scripture's depictions of Mary are confined to the beginning and the end of the Gospels. The majority of the biblical references to Mary center directly on her role as mother. She is mentioned in the genealogy of Jesus; at the Annunciation; at Elizabeth's house, where she is first called "mother of God"; and at the birth of Jesus.

Although Jesus' mother makes very few appearances in sacred Scripture, as compared with St. Peter, for example, indications of Mary's special role in the life of Jesus and in our lives as a people of faith spring readily from the text.

From the Old Testament, which foreshadows her, to Revelation, which alludes to her as the Queen of Heaven, Mary is there as a bright morning star pointing the way to her Son. As the Gospels tell us, Mary is there at the beginning of the Christian era, giving her consent to the Incarnation; she is there at the beginning of Jesus' public ministry, telling him it is time for him to act; and she is there beneath the cross, standing in agony next to John as her Son dies a horrible death.

Although Jesus' mother makes very few appearances in sacred Scripture, indications of Mary's special role in the life of Jesus and in our lives as a people of faith spring readily from the text.

In the Beginning . . .

Nazareth, the town where Jesus was brought up and lived until about the age of thirty, was a humble village, not mentioned in the Old Testament or in Jewish literature. Set in the Lower Galilee region, Nazareth is located in Israel's western hills, an area consisting of some fertile valleys and a number of east-to-west natural ridges, none rising above two thousand feet.

Mary of Nazareth—whose name is written at times in the Hebraic form, Mariam—was a chaste young Jewish girl betrothed to a devout Jewish man, Joseph. The portrait of her in the New Testament is that of a prayerful Jewish woman

MARY IN SCRIPTURE

with very human traits who aspired to follow the practices set by Jewish law and religion. The picture of Mary that emerges through the Gospels is at times powerful and detailed. She celebrates. She suffers. She observes. She prays. She treasures things in her heart and reflects on them.

Long before Mary's soft light ever graced the dusty streets of Nazareth, the prophet Isaiah wrote of her, saying "the Lord himself will give you this sign: the virgin shall be with child, and bear a son, and shall name him Immanuel" (Isaiah 7:14).

Mary is first mentioned by name in the Gospel of Matthew: "Jacob was the father of Joseph the husband of Mary. / It was of her that Jesus who is called the Messiah was born" (1:16). To understand what seems to be a rather casual first appearance of Mary in Scripture, we need to place Matthew 1:16 in the context of the whole of Matthew's first chapter and pull in John 1:1–5.

An important part of getting to know people, especially if we desire intimacy, involves learning their family story. It is in discovering their past that we are able to contextualize their present. Did they come from a rich or poor family? Were they refugees or migrants? Were they formally educated? Was their family large or small? Is their family intact or has it experienced loss? In very different ways, both John and Matthew attempt to convey to the reader a sense of Jesus' family history.

John's opening emphasis is on Jesus' divine family tree:

> In the beginning was the Word;
> the Word was in God's presence,
> and the Word was God.
> He was present to God in the beginning.
> Through him all things came into being,
> and apart from him nothing came to be.
> Whatever came to be in him, found life,
> life for the light of men.
> The light shines on in darkness,
> a darkness that did not overcome it. (John 1:1–5)

What a remarkable family history! Or to put it more accurately, what a remarkable family that created history. John establishes that the Word, who becomes incarnate through Mary, is with God and is God. Without him, we are nothing, because he brought all things into existence. Because of the sin of our original parents, Adam and Eve, we were separated from this most extraordinary of all families. Through the new Adam—Jesus, the Word incarnate—we are reconciled with the eternal family of God. For this to happen, the author of creation entered history as a creature taking on our human nature. Being fully human requires development within a mother's womb and often entails growing to maturity within the context of a family. It was no different for Jesus. And this, Jesus' human setting, is Matthew's emphasis as he opens his Gospel.

Much like a modern genealogist, Matthew recounts the earthly lineage of Jesus, linking him to the Davidic line through Joseph, his legal father. His family tree begins with Abraham, includes Isaac, Jacob, Ruth, David, and Solomon, and ends with his parents, Joseph and Mary—an impressive pedigree for a humble carpenter from Nazareth!

Placed within the context of Matthew 1 and John 1:1–5, Mary's first appearance by name in the Gospels takes on tremendous significance. "It was of [Mary] that Jesus who is called the Messiah was born" (Matthew 1:16). She is not merely the mother of a child born of any royal line but is the mother of a child born into and as the fulfillment of the messianic royal line of David and, before him, Abraham. God's promise to the aged and childless Abraham that his descendants would be more numerous than the stars of the sky (Genesis 15:5) was fulfilled fully through the birth of the Christ child, who came to reconcile all the world with God. In this sense, Mary, the mother of the fully human and fully divine Jesus, is our mother. As members of the Body of Christ, who was birthed into existence through Mary, we are the descendants—the heirs—of the covenant of reconciliation between God and humans.

Matthew and John introduce us to Jesus' human and divine family tree. Next we turn to Luke to get to know Mary more intimately. It is the Gospel of Luke that describes the familiar account of the angel Gabriel's announcement to

Mary that she was to have a child through the intervention of the Holy Spirit:

> In the sixth month, the angel Gabriel was sent from God to a town of Galilee named Nazareth, to a virgin betrothed to a man named Joseph, of the house of David. The virgin's name was Mary. Upon arriving, the angel said to her: "Rejoice, O highly favored daughter! The Lord is with you. Blessed are you among women." She was deeply troubled by his words, and wondered what his greeting meant. The angel went on to say to her: "Do not fear, Mary. You have found favor with God. You shall conceive and bear a son and give him the name Jesus." (Luke 1:26–31)

We return to Matthew for Joseph's side of the story:

> When his mother Mary was engaged to Joseph, but before they lived together, she was found with child through the power of the Holy Spirit. Joseph her husband, an upright man unwilling to expose her to the law, decided to divorce her quietly. Such was his intention when suddenly the angel of the Lord appeared in a dream and said to him: "Joseph, son of David, have no fear about taking Mary as your wife. It is by the Holy Spirit that she has conceived this child. She is to have a son and you are to name him Jesus because he will save his people from their sins." . . .

When Joseph awoke he did as the angel of the Lord
had directed him and received her into his home as his
wife. He had no relations with her at any time before
she bore a son, whom he named Jesus. (Matthew
1:18–21, 24–25)

From these two passages, we get a sense of the drama that is
about to unfold. Before we continue to unravel the story, we
need to more fully introduce Jesus' stepfather, Joseph, and the
legal status of his relationship with Mary at the time of the
Annunciation.

A Jewish Betrothal and the Annunciation

Nothing is said of St. Joseph in Scripture prior to the annunciation by the angel Gabriel to Mary. Tradition, however, has
always described Joseph as a builder and a carpenter from the
town of Nazareth. According to Matthew 1:16 and Luke 1:27,
Joseph was from the royal line of David. Matthew describes
Jesus' relationship to his earthly father by calling him "the
carpenter's son" (13:55), while Luke simply calls him the son
of Joseph (4:22). The Gospel of Mark never mentions Joseph
by name, calling Jesus only "the son of Mary" (6:3). Joseph
makes no appearance during Jesus' ministry in any of the
Gospels, and biblical scholars believe it is likely that he died
before Jesus' baptism in the Jordan. Joseph is remembered as
a chaste, holy, and just man, a faithful Jew who Scripture tells

us had loving compassion for his newly betrothed even when she was found to be with child before they were completely married.

According to biblical scholar Raymond E. Brown, the Jewish custom of betrothal consisted of two steps: a formal exchange of consent before witnesses and the subsequent taking of the bride to the groom's family home. While the term *marriage* is sometimes used to designate the second step, he notes, in terms of legal implications it would more properly be applied to the first step.

> The consent, usually entered into when the girl was between twelve and thirteen years old, would constitute a legally ratified marriage in our terms, since it gave the young man rights over the girl. She was henceforth his wife, and any infringement on his marital rights could be punished as adultery. Yet the wife continued to live at her own family home, usually for about a year. (*The Birth of the Messiah*, 123–24)

Just as it is difficult for us to find the correct word for Mary and Joseph's marital status, it must have been difficult for translators of the New Testament text to find the exact word in Greek to appropriately convey the state in the Jewish matrimonial process that the Evangelists meant when they said that Mary and Joseph were "betrothed." Based on what we know of Jewish custom, however, we can assume that they were between the two steps. As Matthew describes, Mary was found with child when she "was engaged to Joseph, but before they lived together. . . . He had no relations with her at any time before she bore a son, whom he named Jesus" (1:18, 25).

During this time of betrothal, first Mary and then Joseph received visits from an angel. We know that Mary was frightened and "deeply troubled" by this unexpected house call. What did God's beckoning mean for her life? She responded favorably and obediently to God's invitation despite the fact that she was a teenage virgin. She fully trusted that the Lord would work out the numerous religious and cultural problems that would arise from her pregnancy. Joseph, upon learning of her pregnancy, suspected adultery, a crime punishable by death. A man of integrity, he refused to condemn Mary to this fate, preferring to end the matter quietly, but he too was surprised by an angelic visitor, who assured him that his marriage to Mary could go on as planned.

Despite how dramatically they are presented, the factual details of the story of the Annunciation—a betrothed young woman is found with child before she has lived with her husband—do not reflect the scandal of the story. The real scandal of the Annunciation story is that God's love for his people is so great that he chose to touch humanity in the most intimate way. God chose to become one with humanity through his Son, a child who was to be fully human and fully divine. As the angel of the Lord announced to Joseph, "It is by the Holy Spirit that she has conceived this child" (Matthew 1:20). This wondrous transaction with the Creator of the

9

universe is made possible through Mary and because of her consent. Mary, who was "deeply troubled" by the angel's words, must have been frightened by the powerful events that were suddenly transforming her life. But Luke records her ultimate trust in God and her faith-filled response to the angel's announcement: "Mary said: 'I am the servant of the Lord. Let it be done to me as you say'" (Luke 1:38). To commemorate this dialogue between Gabriel and Mary, the church, from its beginnings, has celebrated the feast of the Annunciation on March 25.

In their exchange, Gabriel, declaring that "nothing is impossible for God," also told Mary that her elderly kinswoman Elizabeth was pregnant. Luke narrates Mary's visit to her cousin Elizabeth, who was pregnant with John the Baptist. It is Elizabeth who first calls Mary "the mother of my Lord."

> When Elizabeth heard Mary's greeting, the baby leapt in her womb. Elizabeth was filled with the Holy Spirit and cried out in a loud voice: "Blest are you among women and blest is the fruit of your womb. But who am I that the mother of my Lord should come to me? The moment your greeting sounded in my ears, the baby leapt in my womb for joy. Blest is she who trusted that the Lord's words to her would be fulfilled." (Luke 1:41–45)

This passage is striking for a number of reasons. First, it is the unborn John who first recognizes the greatness of the prize that Mary carries within her womb. Those who approach Christ with the faith of a child will have the eyes to see and the ears to hear. As a mother, Elizabeth is aware of the movements of her child, and as if taking his cue, she comes to understand the significance of Mary's visit. In most cultures—and this Jewish culture would have been no different—the younger woman would have greeted the older woman with respect and acclamation. But in this story it is the elder woman—Elizabeth—who declares her teenage kinswoman blessed, and not just blessed, but uniquely blessed among women.

The first half of the prayer that we call the Hail Mary is actually a combination of the angel Gabriel's greeting,

Hail Mary, full of grace, the Lord is with you

and Elizabeth's proclamation,

Blessed are you among women,
and blessed is the fruit of your womb, Jesus.

The Hail Mary and the rosary will be discussed further in chapter 6, where I discuss Marian prayers.

Mary's canticle, her response to Elizabeth's greeting, is known as the Magnificat, which we recite daily as part of evening prayer:

My being proclaims the greatness of the Lord,
    my spirit finds joy in God my savior.
For he has looked upon his servant in her lowliness;
    all ages to come shall call me blessed.
God who is mighty has done great things for me,
    holy is his name;
His mercy is from age to age
    on those who fear him. (Luke 1:46–50)

The message of this song, notes Kathleen Norris, "is so subversive that for a period during the 1980s the government of Guatemala banned its public recitation." It is

> praise of the God who has blessed two insignificant women in an insignificant region of ancient Judea, and in so doing "has brought down the powerful from their thrones, and lifted up the lowly, has filled the hungry with good things, and sent the rich away empty" (Luke 1:52–3). I later learned that these words echo the song of Hannah in First Samuel, as well as the anguish of the prophets. They are a poetic rendering of a theme that pervades the entire biblical narrative— when God comes into our midst, it is to upset the status quo. (*Amazing Grace*, 117)

Subversive. Bold. Wondrous. This is the scandal of the Annunciation, as proclaimed by Mary and Elizabeth. We believe in a mighty God who chose a lowly woman as the vessel for his humanity, as the means through which his Son would be born into the human world. There is no greater sign of God's mercy and love for his people. Mary recognized in her heart the wonder of it all and proclaimed it in song.

The Birth Narrative

The Gospels of Matthew and Luke are the only two to record the narratives of the birth of Jesus. Just as they emphasize different aspects of Jesus' lineage, these Gospel writers point to two distinct communities who will receive Christ's saving message. Luke points to the shepherds working in the field at night who heard the multitude of heavenly hosts praising God and proclaiming: "This day in David's city a savior has been born to you, the Messiah and Lord. Let this be a sign to you: in a manger you will find an infant wrapped in swaddling clothes. . . . / Glory to God in high heaven, / peace on earth to those on whom his favor rests" (Luke 2:11–12, 14). To the news the shepherds responded, "'Let us go over to Bethlehem and see this event which the Lord has made known to us.' They went in haste and found Mary and Joseph, and the baby lying in the manger; once they saw, they understood what had been told them concerning this child" (Luke 2:15–17). Jesus came to reconcile the chosen people, the Jews, with God. Even before Jesus could speak and thirty years before his public ministry began, we catch a glimpse of

13

the future—it will be the poor and the marginalized in the Jewish community who will flock to the Good Shepherd.

Matthew, on the other hand, foreshadows what the psalms also foreshadowed, that Jesus was to come not only for the Jews but for all of humanity. He reports that "astrologers from the east" traveled to Bethlehem following a star that "they had observed at its rising." The Magi "were overjoyed at seeing the star, and on entering the house, found the child with Mary his mother. They prostrated themselves and did him homage. Then they opened their coffers and presented him with gifts of gold, frankincense, and myrrh" (Matthew 2:10–11). With watchful eyes, even the pagan cultures could come to know Mary's Son as the King of kings.

These first days after Jesus' birth were truly miraculous, with the angelic choirs, shepherds, and wise men coming to adore Jesus. Those who witnessed this pivotal event in history were deeply affected by all that they saw and experienced, but it would be another generation or two before the meaning of these events would begin to be understood. All the while, Mary, who "treasured all these things," continued to "reflect on them in her heart."

With Joseph, Mary carried out the traditional Jewish rituals of circumcision and of presenting their firstborn male in the temple, in accordance with the law of Moses (Luke 2:22). Only Luke records the circumcision of Jesus and the presentation in the temple, where the prophetess Anna and the holy man Simeon witnessed to anyone who would listen that they had seen the Anointed of the Lord. Simeon also blessed Mary and Joseph, St. Luke tells us, and then said only to Mary: "This child is destined to be the downfall and the rise of many in Israel, a sign that will be opposed—and you yourself shall be pierced with a sword—so that the thoughts of many hearts may be laid bare" (2:34–35).

We know from Matthew's account that Herod felt threatened by the Magi's journey and by the prophecy that a king would come from Bethlehem. God protected the holy family, leading them out of the Promised Land and back to Egypt, where they lived as refugees until Herod's death. Upon their return, they settled in Nazareth.

Luke is the only one to record the episode of the boy Jesus in the temple, a parenting incident from what is often described as the "hidden life" of Jesus, his life with his family at Nazareth before his public ministry. When Jesus was twelve, Luke writes, Mary and Joseph traveled to Jerusalem for the feast of the Passover, as was their custom:

> As they were returning at the end of the feast, the child Jesus remained behind unknown to his parents. Thinking he was in the party, they continued their journey for a day, looking for him among their relatives and acquaintances.
>
> Not finding him, they returned to Jerusalem in search of him. On the third day they came upon him in the

temple sitting in the midst of the teachers, listening to them and asking them questions. . . . His mother said to him: "Son, why have you done this to us? You see that your father and I have been searching for you in sorrow." He said to them: "Why did you search for me? Did you not know I had to be in my Father's house?" But they did not grasp what he said to them. (Luke 2:43–47, 48–50)

It is not difficult for me to understand and relate to the anxiety that Mary and Joseph must have felt when they realized that their Son was not with them—and that they did not know where he was. It is a parent's worst nightmare. I know all too well the rapid thumping in the chest that Mary must have felt as she looked for Jesus, "searching for [him] in sorrow." And I understand the mixture of relief and bewilderment that Mary must have experienced when she finally found her "lost" Son. As a mother, Mary must have also felt perplexed by Jesus' extremely calm reaction to her question "Why have you done this to us?" Yet as Scripture notes, Mary listened and "kept all these things in memory" (Luke 2:51), trusting in God's plan even when she did not understand.

The Rest of the Story

From this time and until the beginning of his public ministry, when Jesus was about thirty, Scripture is silent, except to say that "he went down with them then [from Jerusalem], and came to Nazareth, and was obedient to them" (Luke 2:51).

Mary is present at the Annunciation, at the Nativity, and at every significant event in her Son's early life. She watches him grow to manhood, and when the time comes for Jesus to enter his public ministry, Mary is there in a very active way. She who gave birth to the Messiah gives birth to his public ministry by encouraging him to come to the aid of a soon-to-be-embarrassed wedding party. As she has done throughout subsequent history, Mary intercedes with her Son on behalf of someone in need.

In the Gospel of John, the first mention of Mary is in the story of the wedding at Cana, a village near Nazareth, although Mary is referred to simply as "Jesus' mother."

On the third day there was a wedding at Cana in Galilee, and the mother of Jesus was there. Jesus and his disciples had likewise been invited to the celebration. At a certain point the wine ran out, and Jesus' mother told him, "They have no more wine." Jesus replied, "Woman, how does this concern of yours involve me? My hour has not yet come." His mother instructed those waiting on table, "Do whatever he tells you." . . . Jesus performed this first of his signs at Cana in Galilee. Thus did he reveal his glory, and his disciples believed in him. (John 2:1–5, 11)

MARY IN SCRIPTURE

This first miracle portrays the esteem in which Jesus holds his mother as well as the godly self-respect lived out by Mary. Wine in Jewish lore was a sign not only of God's loving gifts to human beings, but also of divine wisdom, and it was used in Jewish rites of purification. Mary observed the situation at the wedding and discovered a need. The Evangelist notes that it was Mary who requested the miracle. Jesus responded with hesitation, aware that turning water into wine would begin his journey of salvation, a journey that would someday lead to wine being turned into blood. Mary spoke her opinion with confidence—speaking for the last time in Scripture—and Jesus, her Son, acceded to her request.

This event is certainly not without significance in John's presentation. Just as she had done after the shepherds' visit in the birth narrative, Mary treasured and held these things in her heart. Mary "may not have understood what he said of himself," explains Scripture scholar Raymond Brown, "she may even have reproached him; but she is not unresponsive to the mystery that surrounds him. Her lack of understanding is not permanent; for the fact that she keeps with concern such events in her heart is by way of preparation for a future understanding as a member of the believing community (Acts 1:14)." By stressing Mary's memory of the things that happened and her desire to understand them, Brown notes, Luke is giving us "a perceptive theological insight into history: there was continuity from the infant Jesus to the boy Jesus to the Jesus of the ministry to the risen Jesus; and when

Christian disciples like Mary believed in Jesus as God's Son after the resurrection, they were finding adequate expression for institutions that had begun long before" (*Birth*, 494).

The next direct reference to Mary in the Gospels is in Jesus' own words, when he compares his relationship with his followers to his relationship with his mother:

> He was still addressing the crowds when his mother and his brothers appeared outside to speak with him. Someone said to him, "Your mother and your brothers are standing out there and they wish to speak to you." He said to the one who had told him, "Who is my mother? Who are my brothers?" Then, extending his hand toward his disciples, he said, "There are my mother and my brothers. Whoever does the will of my heavenly Father is brother and sister and mother to me." (Matthew 12:46–50; see also Mark 3:31–35)

Many Protestants use this passage to downplay the role of Mary, even suggesting that Jesus was ignoring his mother, preferring those in his company to the woman who gave birth to him and raised him. But looking only at these lines takes the passage out of context. True, Jesus suggests that the concept of kinship transcends blood relationships. But pause on his words "whoever does the will of my heavenly Father is . . . mother to me." Mary is the embodiment of this yes to God.

All generations will call Mary blessed because of her willingness to say yes to the most important question ever asked: Will you incarnate the Word inside of you, not just for yourself and your personal salvation but for the salvation of all the world? Far from distancing himself from Mary in the above passage, Jesus actually holds her out as a model of Christian kinship with himself. The depiction of Mary in Scripture is above all the picture of a woman of courage who trusted her Creator's design for her life, all the way to the foot of the cross.

It is only in John's testimony of Jesus' crucifixion and death that Jesus once again addresses his mother as "woman," as he did at Cana. Our culture might find this term odd, but it was considered entirely courteous and even a term of honor in Jesus' day.

After the soldiers had crucified Jesus and divided his garments, John tells us:

> Near the cross of Jesus there stood his mother, his mother's sister, Mary the wife of Clopas, and Mary Magdalene. Seeing his mother there with the disciple whom he loved, Jesus said to his mother, "Woman, there is your son." In turn he said to his disciple, "There is your mother." From that hour onward, the disciple took her into his care. (19:25–27)

The fact that Jesus addressed his mother as "woman" both at the Crucifixion and at the miracle at Cana is considered by scholars to be symbolic. At the Crucifixion, "the hour" that Jesus had noted at Cana has now come. Mary is here given the role of spiritual mother to all the faithful, represented by the beloved disciple. Since the Gospel of John is highly charged with symbols, scholars remind us that we should not see in this gesture a mere sign of Jesus' filial love, an effort to take care of his mother, who would now be left alone. It is an hour of birth pangs. At the moment when new life is coming into the world, we are given another mother, a new mother of all the living.

A final reference to Mary, found in the Acts of the Apostles, lists her among the apostles gathered in the community in Jerusalem between the time of the ascension of Jesus and Pentecost.

> After [the Ascension] they returned to Jerusalem from the mount called Olivet near Jerusalem—a mere sabbath's journey away. Entering the city, they went to the upstairs room where they were staying. . . . Together they devoted themselves to constant prayer. There were some women in their company, and Mary the mother of Jesus, and his brothers. (Acts 1:12–14)

The day of Pentecost came and "found them gathered in one place." It is assumed that "they" refers to the group previously mentioned in Acts 1:13–14, which included the Blessed Virgin Mary.

Suddenly from up in the sky there came a noise like a strong, driving wind which was heard all through the house where they were seated. Tongues as of fire appeared, which parted and came to rest on each of them. All were filled with the Holy Spirit. (Acts 2:2–4)

Mary brings Christ into the world and remains with his disciples even after Jesus' death on the cross. Although the New Testament canon that grew out of early church tradition includes few references to Mary, there is enough presented on Mary and on the nature of her Son for the church to ponder in its heart as even now it tries to grasp the meaning of the Incarnation.

The depiction of Mary in Scripture is above all the picture of a woman of courage who trusted her Creator's design for her life, all the way to the foot of the cross.

I sing of a maiden
That is matchless;
King of all kings,
For her son she chose.
He came all so still
Where his mother was,
As dew in April
That falleth on the grass.
He came all so still
To his mother's bowr,
As dew in April
That falleth on the flower.
He came all so still
Where his mother lay,
As dew in April
That falleth on the spray.
Mother and maiden
Was never none but she;
Well may such a lady
[God's] mother be.

—ANONYMOUS, FOURTEENTH CENTURY
"I Sing of a Maiden"

CHAPTER TWO

Mary, the First Christian

The First Yes: What Does It Mean for Us?

On my first visit to Mary's hometown of Nazareth and to the Church of the Annunciation, built on the traditional site of Mary's first encounter with the archangel Gabriel, I parted from my tour group to look for a Mass. It should not be difficult, I reasoned, *in this amalgamation of churches and chapels, to find a place where Mass is being celebrated.* I confidently strolled down Pilgrims' Way, and in no time I was able to join a community of believers gathered in the main sanctuary of the Church of St. Joseph, next to the Church of the Annunciation.

As I "listened"—in Italian!—to the long homily that cool spring day, I was suddenly overwhelmed by the awareness that here, two thousand years before, in this unimportant village in Lower Galilee, an unimportant young woman had allowed God to be born within her. It was here that Mary said that first incredible, wondrous, and world-changing yes, not knowing exactly what her yes meant or where it would take her, but fully trusting in a God whose presence was obviously central in her life.

This became a vivid and concrete reality for me, and in what St. Anthony of the Desert describes as "real prayer"—that which we do not understand—I heard the words "be born in me" leap out from my heart as tears surprised my eyes. There are no words to aptly describe that type of spiritual experience. I simply and clearly recognized the Word's presence within me. I felt, in a spiritual sense, pregnant with God's reality. And as the young teenager Mary of Nazareth had, I too said yes to God in my life that day in a unique and real way.

Mary of Nazareth is clearly the first Christian. With that first yes to the angel Gabriel, she was the first to welcome Jesus into her life, to acknowledge him as the Son of God. It is true that Mary carried the Lord, the Son of God, in her womb, but as St. Augustine says of Mary, "she conceived Him in her heart before she conceived Him in the flesh." As the mother of an awesome foursome (one boy and three girls), I can easily relate to the description, the image and the symbolism, of being "pregnant with God." This idea of allowing God to be born within us, in our hearts, is of the essence of who we are as Christians.

As the first person to say yes to Christ's presence in this world, Mary can be a wonderful example for us. In the middle of the fear, anxiety, and confusion that this virgin had to feel when she was told that she would be pregnant with God's Son, Mary opened her heart and aligned herself with God's will for her life. This is something that is asked of every believer, man and woman alike.

There is no way I can sufficiently underscore what this incredible act of faith means to me. I want to do this too. I want to freely and intentionally say yes to Christ being born in me. In order to gain the courage to do this, I can recall specific times in my life when I have felt deep within me that presence of Life and Word, particularly at moments of great darkness and pain or in singular instances of grace, as I did that day in Nazareth. But how can God continue to be born within me daily? And what does it mean for me to say yes?

As long as we are alive, we are all on a faith journey, a lifelong pilgrimage. Whether or not we acknowledge that God is with us on that journey, God does, in fact, walk beside us. Whether or not we realize that our searching for truth is a search for God doesn't change the reality that it is Truth that we seek and Truth that we will find.

"Seek and you shall find" is more than a catchy Bible phrase. It is a promise that if we seek God, we will, indeed, find God. But the words sometimes become the problem. When we allow ourselves to be truly honest with ourselves as we gain more experience of life, each one of us, regardless of our age or our social, economic, or ethnic background, feels a yearning inside. That yearning is God's quiet call.

No words can accurately or rationally explain this yearning. Often, too often, the yearning feels like a painful void, and so we try to fill this gap inside us and to silence the nameless wanting by whatever means possible—by acquiring material goods; participating in exciting, adrenaline-pumping events; filling up our days with people or things that we can obsess over. Yet the quiet call remains and patiently waits for us to stop and be quiet enough to hear it.

Ultimately, it is grace that first allows us to say yes to God, as Mary did, even when we do not understand the significance of that decision. When we stop our obsessing and our busyness long enough to acknowledge that we still feel empty inside, we hear God's quiet whisper. And in faith, we say yes, not knowing or understanding how this will change us or where it will take us. It is grace that reminds us that God wants us to find him.

God wants us to realize that we are, indeed, pregnant with Love. Christ is already there. As we develop spiritually, we slowly come to grasp this spiritual pregnancy, the gift of the Incarnation, and what it means for us, in ever deeper ways. Thankfully, this mystery unfolds before us in small steps, in God's time, so as not to overwhelm us. God does not lead us immediately from total darkness to total and perfect light. Such a sudden change would undoubtedly blind us. It would mean death to our eyes in a physical sense and death to our souls in a spiritual sense. In his infinite mercy, God allows Christ to be birthed in the world and in each of our hearts in a way analogous to the rising of the sun, allowing the pupils of our souls the time needed to adjust as the light continues to grow.

The Gift of the Ordinary

Although she knew Jesus more intimately than we do, Mary shares with every one of us the tribulations of a personal faith-walk with the Lord—the doubts and confusion, the pain and heartache of life, as well as, ultimately, the confident trust in salvation and eternal life. None of us has a perfect understanding of what it means to be a follower of Christ, and neither did Mary. Gabriel's revelation that her Son was to be the Son of God and that he would reign forever must have seemed absolutely inconceivable. Her Son was to be the Messiah.

With her cooperation, "the divine nature and the nature of a servant were to be united in one person so that the Creator of time might be born in time, and he through whom all things were made might be brought forth in their midst" (St. Leo the Great, reprinted in the Office of the Readings, December 17). In this profound way, Mary did know from the beginning her Son's godly purpose in life. But she could not yet grasp the ramifications of that great mystery.

I find great comfort in knowing that Mary experienced mystery in her life. This is the same mystery that we, as Christians, live out daily, hoping that we can learn to understand God's vision and desire for our life, what it's all about. Mary did not say yes only once to

29

God. Indeed, her entire life was a testimony to living faithfully with the Word. We know she said yes freely at the Annunciation. But she also said yes to raising a child who was the Son of God. She said yes every time she accompanied him during his ministry. She said yes when she saw him suffer and die on the cross. And she said yes when the Holy Spirit came to her and to the apostles at Pentecost.

Mary did not say yes only once to God. Her entire life was a testimony to living faithfully with the Word.

As a young, unwed, pregnant mother, Mary's life was anything but easy. And it is here that we can meet Mary, the mother of Jesus, not because she understood everything, but because she was a woman who said yes daily. As Mary did, each of us comes to realize that beyond the original decision to follow Christ, there will continue to be unforeseen events, choices, and circumstances that will require us to renew our commitment. Just as it can be consoling to realize, for example, that all married couples will continue to experience things that will necessitate the renewal of their marriage vows in small, daily, concrete ways, so must we be consoled by continuing to choose Christ in the details of our everyday lives. It can be helpful to realize that Mary experienced this first and can thus both encourage and console us in our daily struggles.

Amid the sacred and glorious events and miracles, Mary of Nazareth remained a young mother and wife. As a mother, I know how motherhood affects the very fabric of a person. Not only is a woman's physical appearance modified forever by pregnancy and childbirth, but there is also an invisible yet undeniable mark left on her spirit by that experience. A miracle of life takes place within a woman's body. A human life, known by God even before the moment of conception, is born of her, through her, making her all at once and forever a mother.

Mary knew Jesus as only a mother can know the child she carries within her womb. As she felt the child move within her, she must have wondered how the mystery of his life would be played out. After his birth, as she nursed him from her breasts for the first time, she undoubtedly relished the miracle of holding a child that just hours before had lived inside her. I know I did. As woman and mother, Mary was truly human.

In her characteristically practical and charming way, St. Thérèse of Lisieux explained in a letter how she envisioned the very human life of Mary. Thérèse observed:

> It is easy to deduce that her life both in Nazareth and later on, was quite ordinary. Everything took place as things occur in our own lives. The Blessed Virgin is

31

sometimes pictured as if she were unapproachable. We should realize on the contrary that it is possible to imitate her by practicing her hidden virtues. She lived a life of faith common to all of us and we should prove this from what we are told in the pages of the Gospel. The Blessed Virgin is the Queen of heaven and earth, quite true, but she is more mother than queen. (Jamart, 277)

More mother than queen—now that is a Mary of Nazareth I can relate to!

When I picture the Virgin Mary, I like to envision her in her family's simple kitchen, cooking their favorite meal or perhaps baking bread. I can see her holding hands with the toddler Jesus, on her way to the market through the narrow, busy streets of their hometown. I love the image of her lying next to Jesus at night, this Son she loved with her whole heart, and playing with his hair as she tells him stories about her family, her ancestors, and the prophets.

As I did with my own babies, Mary nursed Jesus and helped him to take his first steps. As we did with our son and daughters, she and Joseph bathed baby Jesus and played with him and sang him to sleep with their own special lullabies. As we do with our children, Mary taught her Son about her faith through stories and through her example. And Mary struggled, as I still do, with separation as she let her Son go away with friends—the apostles—to live out his destiny.

Mary often did not understand God's plans, as is evident in the Gospel story of a young Jesus lost in the temple. After frantically searching for her Son for three days, she finds him preaching in the temple and chastises him: "My child, why have you done this to us? See how worried your father and I have been" (see Luke 2:48). Jesus looks at her and replies, "'Did you not know that I must be busy with my Father's affairs?' But they did not understand what he meant" (see Luke 2:49–50).

This living mystery of our Christianity calls each one of us to embrace the unknown in our lives, as well as the pain and suffering, healing and forgiveness, growth and reconciliation in ourselves and in others. Yet, thank God, we do not have to know or see the full picture of how this is to play out. It would be too much if we did know. We are only called to be, like Mary, willing to embrace God's will with an open heart and to ask Jesus for the courage to live out this desire daily.

It makes sense that Mary's understanding of the Incarnation, like ours, unfolded over time. She continued to say yes to God at every step of living out the mystery, through the daily and ordinary events in life as well as through the major events as they evolved. When the angel Gabriel first appeared to her, Mary could not have imagined the passion and death of her Son. She knew that Jesus was destined for greatness, but she could not have known the cost—the agony of watching her Son die. And even there, at the foot of the cross, in the greatest pain a mother can ever endure, Mary

MARY, THE FIRST CHRISTIAN

trusted that this mystery too would unfold as part of God's plan of salvation.

There is nothing effortless about a mother who chooses to proclaim her faith in God while holding the lifeless body of her son in her arms, the same child she once caressed and cradled when he was a baby. Yet this is the meaning of faith for a Christian, the call of a believer—to trust in God, a good God who loves us and cares for us, especially during the times when we can't see Love with our eyes or understand Life with our minds.

Mary's incomplete understanding of the mystery of her Son's life helps us to understand our own Christian walk. When Mary said yes to God, when she agreed to conceive the Word and allow the Word to become incarnate, she did so in a blind affirmation of faith. She agreed to submit to God's will without knowing the path that lay before her. She must have known that many would not believe the story of the virgin birth, casting suspicion on her character if not stones on her body. But she could not have known that a yes would mean refugee status, rejection of her Son in his own hometown, the exhilaration of miracles and crowds, and seeming humiliation and defeat of her Son at the hands of the Sanhedrin and the Roman procurator. She had been told that her Son would reign as King forever. Did she have moments of doubt as the story unfolded in horrible and tragic ways that were beyond her imagination? Probably. But

Mary persevered, choosing faith and faithfulness to her Son and to his Father.

So it is with us. We hear God's voice in our hearts and we choose to respond blindly: "Be born in me!" We make a commitment to follow Christ and to live as part of his Body, the church, but we have yet to fully understand the mystery of the Incarnation and what it means for our lives. Mary's yes to perfect Love in her life is the first and most important model for each of us as followers of Christ. The dawn from on high is breaking upon us to lead us out of darkness. Following Mary's lead, we must, during each phase of our faith journey—especially in the middle of ordinary life—ponder the mystery of the Incarnation in our hearts (Luke 2:19, 51) and trust that the Messiah will continually enter our being, body and soul, to transform our lives.

Mary's incomplete understanding of the mystery of her Son's life helps us to understand our own Christian walk.

Mary's Command: "Do Whatever He Tells You"

The word *obey* comes from the Latin *oboedire,* meaning "to hear or listen to." If a disciple of Jesus, as the Gospel of Luke tells us, is someone who both hears the word of God and keeps it (Luke 11:28), Mary is, without a doubt, the first and most perfect disciple. To obey in faith, the Catholic Catechism states, is "to submit freely to the word that has been heard, because its truth is guaranteed by God, who is Truth itself." In this sense, there is no doubt that Mary is the "most perfect embodiment" of this obedience (Catechism, 144).

For most of us, however, the word *obedience* evokes a negative, and even oppressive, image—a burden rather than something we readily desire. We say we don't want someone telling us what to do, what to think, or how to live; we want to be individuals, not obedient drones without minds of our own. We boldly declare that we want to be free and unfairly set obedience at the other end of the spectrum from this aspiration. It's ironic, then, that we pay so much attention to the latest fashions; that we read with great interest what experts tell us is the right way to invest our money or build our careers; and that we know exactly what is lauded as the latest technological fad, the highest-rated TV show, or the most popular movie. Is this true independence or the modern equivalent of bondage? For human beings who declare that what we want most of all is to be freestanding individuals, we certainly seem to be extremely in tune with what society—or our friends—tells us we should be or want. This can't be true freedom.

At the beginning of the Gospel of John, we hear that "In the beginning was the Word; / the Word was in God's presence, / and the Word was God" (1:1). When the time came for this Word to enter history in human form, Mary was there, willingly and obediently responding to God's call.

While the Jewish people of her day hoped for the promised Messiah, this poor Jewish teenager, living far from the cultural and religious center of her people, already knew the Messiah in the most intimate way. Long before John the Baptist began his ministry of preparing the people for the coming of the Messiah, Mary already knew the Messiah. And Mary listened. She obeyed, in the full and original sense of that word, and "treasured all these things and reflected on them in her heart" (Luke 2:19).

God, the Creator of the universe, wants us to be free. After all, he created us in his image, to be holy in his eyes. As the prophet Isaiah reminds us, God called each of us by name. God declared us "precious in [God's] eyes / and glorious" (43:4). God called each of us "from birth." "From my mother's womb he gave me my name. . . . / I am made glorious in the sight of the Lord" (Isaiah 49:1, 5). As with the pattern of each simple yet magnificent snowflake, our Creator took delight in making each of us unique. God desires each of us to have this self-awareness, this realization of our uniqueness.

My friend Judy defines the secret of life in this way, as truly becoming aware of our own unique talents. When we learn and accept what our talents are, we can understand the reason for our existence as a personal gift to this world. God wants us and needs us to learn who we are in God's image, to become aware of what makes Maria or John or Michael or Helen unparalleled in the world. To know with our whole being that we do not need a person to tell us we are unique, or a product to make us uniquely special—this is true freedom. This awareness also demands that we learn to listen, to hear in the stillness of our hearts the voice of the One who calls each of us by name.

True freedom, the kind of freedom that is born out of listening and allows us to recognize the uniqueness of who we are, the type of freedom that gives us the courage to open our hearts and say yes in obedience to the God who created us, may seem to some like an oxymoron. How can we be free and obedient at the same time? But Mary offers me an example of what this means through her life and her actions. She had the courage to say yes to God's will for her life in the midst of fear and confusion. I know how that feels.

She also offers me a framework, a blueprint for how to live out this faithful obedience. In chapter 2 of John, we hear the story of Mary, Jesus, and his disciples attending an ordinary celebration, a wedding at Cana in Galilee. Mary, the first among them to become aware of the predicament that the bride and groom would soon find themselves in, said to Jesus, "They have no more wine." At first, Jesus responded to his mother that his "hour had not yet come," indicating that it was not yet time for a sign or a miracle. But Mary did not budge. With complete self-assurance, she simply turned to those in charge and pointed to Jesus, saying, "Do whatever he tells you." As she does over and over in all things, Mary points us to Jesus and reminds us how we are to live out this decision to be followers of Christ: we must do whatever Jesus tells us.

A Contemporary Example: Edith Stein

One of the Catholic Church's newest saints, the Jewish convert and Carmelite martyr Edith Stein, recognized in Mary the perfect fulfillment of what it means to be a Christian, a follower of Jesus. Mary is above all the handmaid of the Lord, Stein wrote, allowing God's will to be done in her life through her own surrender. "[Mary] welcomed [Jesus] from God's hands; she lays Him back into God's hands by dedicating Him in the Temple and by being with Him at the crucifixion." As the follower of Jesus Christ and vessel of His life, noted Stein, Mary was, indeed, the first Christian (*Essays on Woman*, 47).

Edith Stein is herself a great example of the unpredictable and improbable things that happen when a person opens up her heart to God and to God's Love. Born into a German Jewish family at the turn of the twentieth century, Edith Stein lived in a festering political world that tried to dictate and define who she was—and who she wasn't—by demeaning and confining labels. She was a woman in a man's world, an educated person in an increasingly industrial and military society, and a person of Jewish origins in Nazi Germany.

The youngest daughter in a large, close-knit Jewish family, Stein fought her way through phenomenological philosophy at the university, all the while searching for "truth." Just a few years before Hitler took power, Stein became a noted and prolific German philosopher, though she was never allowed to teach at the university level, first because she was a woman, then eventually because of her Jewishness. Throughout her life, Stein remained deeply concerned with truth, culture, freedom, and how to live a life of purpose in a modern world. She searched, as most of us do, for something to complete the unanswered questions whispering in her heart.

Then the unexpected happened. Shortly before turning thirty, Stein picked up a book entitled *Life* from a friend's library while on an overnight visit. It was that night, reading the life of St. Teresa of Ávila, that Edith Stein could finally proclaim: "This is truth!" A few months later, Stein was baptized in the Catholic Church, and eleven years after that she joined the cloistered Discalced Carmelites, taking on the religious name Sister Teresa Benedicta of the Cross.

To say that these choices were improbable for Edith Stein is an understatement. But to look at only the surface of her life is to miss the heart of her story. Stein loved truth and yearned for it. She could not understand or define or predict what this meant, but throughout her life, she remained open to finding truth. God listened to the deep desires of her heart even when she didn't know or understand them and even before she believed that God was there. This is God's promise to each of us. If we seek him, he will let us find him!

After she became a Christian, Stein regarded Mary, a fellow Jewish woman, as the perfect example of what it means to shine with the awareness of being a child of God and, in that love, to choose to listen and to obey. A relationship with Mary of Nazareth was as natural to Stein as one with her own birth mother, with whom she was very close. Stein saw in Mary, the first person to choose Christ, a spiritual model for all who make a deliberate choice to follow Jesus. As Mary did, Edith Stein desired to live a life of total and trusting surrender to the God who led her to Truth and Life, and her entire life came to embody the truth that she had sought for so long.

> My life begins anew each morning and ends each evening; beyond that I have no plans or intentions; that is, it may be part of one's daily duties to plan ahead, but one must never worry about the next day. . . . If you put yourself completely into the hands of the Lord, you can trust that you are being guided safely. What you surrender to Him is never lost; it is preserved, purified, and elevated and balanced to the correct proportions. . . . Thus it has to be; one must put oneself totally in God's hands, without any human support; then the feeling of security becomes all the more profound and beautiful. (*An Edith Stein Daybook*, 8)

No matter how many lectures on how many intricate topics she was asked to present, Stein remarked in a letter to a Benedictine sister friend and former student, "Basically, it is always a small, simple truth that I have to express: How to go about living at the Lord's hand" (*Self-Portrait in Letters, 1916–1942*, 87).

We are all, regardless of our vocation, called to the imitation of Christ. As Christians, we are challenged in a unique and personal way to bring Christ to the world through our love, our actions, our decisions, and our attitudes. Six years after her conversion, Edith Stein wrote to a friend in Munich:

> Immediately before, and for a good while after my conversion, I was of the opinion that to lead a religious life meant one had to give up all that was secular and to live totally immersed in thoughts of the Divine. But gradually I realized that something else is asked of us in this world and that . . . one may not sever the connection with the world. I even believe that the deeper one is drawn to God, the more one must "go out of oneself"; that is, one must go to the world in order to carry the divine life into it." (*Self-Portrait in Letters, 1916–1942*, 54)

Learning what it means to listen to God begins with prayer, both personal and communal. It is in prayer that I sit before God, the Creator, as I am—not as I wish I could be. It is in prayer that my brokenness is healed and I am made whole. Prayer makes me real.

It is in prayer that I find the courage to open myself and allow the Word to become flesh within my heart and, with

42

Mary, to proclaim, "I am the handmaid of the Lord. Let it be done to me according to your word." And Edith Stein, like the rest of us, understood that it is in prayer that we gain the courage, the strength, and the vision to live as Christians. While we may not know the details of Mary's prayer life, we know that she had an intimate and real relationship with God. As Mary no doubt did, Stein struggled with the real details of how to live out in the world, in daily life, the truth she had come to know in her heart. As Stein described in a letter to a Dominican sister friend, her own "recipe" for life was centered on prayer, quiet prayer, where one learns what it means to live in the knowledge that God is in us.

> Religion is not something to be relegated to a quiet corner or for a few festive hours, but rather . . . it must be the root and basis of all life: and that, not merely for a few chosen ones, but for every true Christian. . . . The only essential is that one finds, first of all, a quiet corner in which one can communicate with God as though there were nothing else, and that must be done daily. It seems to me the best time is in the early morning hours before we begin our daily work; furthermore, [it is also essential] that one accepts one's particular mission there, preferably for each day, and does not make one's own choice. Finally, one is to consider oneself totally as an instrument, especially with regard to the abilities one uses to perform one's

special tasks, in our case, e.g., intellectual ones. We are
to see them as something used, not by us, but by God
in us. (*Self-Portrait in Letters, 1916–1942*, 54–55)

Mary is, indeed, the ultimate example of how to live that
challenge, and Edith Stein understood what this meant,
especially for women. "Mary's motherhood is the archetype
of all motherhood; like her, every human mother should be
mother with all her soul, in order to pour the entire wealth
of her soul into the soul of her child" (*An Edith Stein
Daybook*, 98).

Stein always looked to Mary for guidance and as a model
for the spiritual life.

Maternity itself is glorified through her. Every woman
who wants to fulfill her destiny must look to Mary as
ideal. . . . That woman who, everywhere she goes,
brings along with her the Savior and enkindles love for
Him will fulfill her feminine vocation in its purest
form. Basically . . . woman's intrinsic value lies in
making room within herself for God's being and
works. (*Essays on Woman*, 41)

There is no better example or guide for living out this choice
for Christ in the world than Mary, who made room for the
Word of God to become flesh within her.

As Kathleen Norris writes:

I used to feel the dissonance whenever I heard Mary described as both Virgin and Mother; as this seemed to set an impossible standard for any woman. But this was narrow-minded on my part. What Mary does is to show me how I indeed can be both virgin and mother. Virgin to the extent that I remain "one-in-myself," able to come to things with newness of heart; mother to the extent that I forget myself in the nurture and service of others, embracing the ripeness of maturity that this requires. This Mary is a gender-bender; she could do the same for any man. (*Amazing Grace*, 122)

It is not difficult to see why Edith Stein saw Mary as a model, as the first and foremost Christian. Like the Jewish woman from Nazareth, Edith Stein made tremendous and difficult choices in her life that intrinsically changed the way she perceived and lived in the world. Stein had the courage to recognize Christ, and she responded to Christ's call within her heart, not knowing exactly where this would lead her. As Mary did, Stein said yes to Christ's being born within her, and she trusted in God's divine providence in her life, regardless of the circumstances and labels and restrictions the world placed on her.

Stein's life was cut short by people whose evil intent and vision were more violent than we can humanly comprehend. In August 1942, Edith Stein and her sister Rosa were arrested by the Nazis at the Carmelite convent in Echt, the Netherlands, where they had been moved for safety. They were then taken to Auschwitz, where they were both killed. Stein was canonized a saint in the Catholic Church by Pope John Paul II in October 1998. At her canonization Mass, the pope remarked:

> At the beginning [Stein] devoted herself to freedom. For a long time Edith Stein was a seeker. Her mind never tired of searching and her heart always yearned for hope. . . . Eventually she was rewarded: she seized the truth. Or better: she was seized by it. Then she discovered that truth had a name: Jesus Christ. From that moment on, the incarnate Word was her One and All. . . . May the new saint be an example to us in our commitment to serve freedom, in our search for the truth. May her witness constantly strengthen the bridge of mutual understanding between Jews and Christians.

Every single choice we make in life will lead either to the Truth we profess or away from it. Like Mary, Edith Stein was a passionate, honest woman who completely opened up her heart to God and to God's vision for her life. And she chose, consistently and faithfully, to walk toward the Truth that had opened her eyes and touched her heart. Their example is the legacy that Stein and Mary leave for us.

One Final Thought on Mary, the First Christian

As a church and as individuals, when we talk about Mary, we too often sound like teenagers embarrassed to be seen with their parents in public. We act as though talking about Mary is taking something away from Jesus, her Son. What a silly proposition, to think that we can in any way diminish God's vision of salvation by acknowledging the woman whom God chose as a partner in bringing about the Incarnation! In reality, by using a simple woman from Nazareth as the instrument through which he came into the world, God gave us a marvelous gift.

Mary was a daughter, a wife, a mother. Unlike the Son to whom she gave birth, Mary was not divine. She was completely and totally human, as we are. Mary wanted to learn what it meant to love God through her life. She was afraid. She prayed for courage. She felt anguish and pain. Her heart leaped with joy. She took care of a baby. She tried to be a good wife. She was Jesus' first and primary teacher. She saw truth, mystery, and love and treasured them in her heart. She cooked and cleaned. She prayed at the synagogue. She encouraged and comforted her Son and even urged him to recognize and act in compassion toward others in need, as at the wedding feast in Cana.

Unlike the Son to whom she gave birth, Mary was not divine. She was completely and totally human, as we are.

There is no better example for us of what it means to be in an honest and intimate relationship with God, our Creator, than Mary. There is no better person to show us what it means to live out a "yes" life, choosing to bring God into the world every day. No other person can accompany us on the Christian walk in the way that Mary can. To paraphrase theologian Hans Urs von Balthasar, Mary, as the first Christian, shows what God's grace is capable of realizing in each one of us.

Salvation to all that will is nigh,
That All, which alwayes is All every where,
Which cannot sinne, and yet all sinnes must beare,
Which cannot die, yet cannot chuse but die,
Loe, faithfull Virgin, yeelds himselfe to lye
In prison, in thy wombe; and though he there
Can take no sinne, nor thou give, yet he'will weare
Taken from thence, flesh, which deaths force may
                                        trie.
Ere by the spheares time was created, thou
Wast in his minde, who is thy Sonne, and Brother,
Whom thou conceiv'st, conceiv'd; yea thou art now
Thy Makers maker, and thy Fathers mother,
Thou'hast light in darke; and shutst in little roome,
Immensity cloysterd in thy deare wombe.

—*JOHN DONNE*
"Annunciation"

CHAPTER THREE

Mary in History

Tradition . . . Tradition!

As a Cuban-born woman who has lived in the United States for most of my life, I am deeply aware of the critical significance of tradition. Without the family stories, the shared memories, and the days of remembrance and commemoration, passing down any form of Cuban culture to my own children would be impossible. Much as the early Christian church relied on oral communication and personal sharing to live out and share their faith from generation to generation, the Cuban community in exile—like many ethnic communities living in today's world without a physical place to define their identity—must depend on tradition and personal stories to survive and endure. Without people sharing from the heart that which is important to their personhood, that which they have recognized as having truth and value, there would be no culture, no tradition. Such is also the case with church tradition.

In order to fully appreciate the importance of tradition in the early Christian church, it is essential to realize that the church had already spread throughout the entire Roman Empire before a single book of the New Testament had been written. Before there were Gospels or Epistles, in fact, there were already many martyrs of the Christian faith. To the early Christians, the witness preached by the apostles was a continuation of Jesus' commission to "go, therefore, and make disciples of all the nations. / Baptize them in the name / of the Father, / and of the Son, / and of the Holy Spirit. / Teach them to carry out everything I have commanded you" (Matthew 28:19–20).

"When finally the Gospels were written, they recorded a tradition; they did not create it," writes Archbishop Fulton J. Sheen in *The World's First Love: Mary, Mother of God.* "It was already there. After a while men had decided to put in writing this living tradition and voice. . . . The Gospels did not start the Church; the Church started the Gospels. The Church did not come out of the Gospels; the Gospels came out of the Church. The Church preceded the New Testament, not the New Testament the Church" (53). Unquestionably, scriptural references to Mary yield only the barest outlines of her blessed life. Yet from the beginning, the early church retained and passed on her story in paintings, in stone carvings, in sculptures, in cathedral murals. It is through this collection of visually represented memories that the body of believers has learned much of Mary's story. We discover Mary's parents, Anne and Joachim. We see Mary as a toddler and Mary learning to read at her mother's side. We contemplate angels removing Mary's body from the tomb. We ascertain through an artist's rendition that Mary sat beside her Son as she was crowned the Queen of Heaven.

The memory of the Mystical Body of Christ, which we call church tradition, lives on and is passed along from person to person. It began with the memories of the apostles and the writings of early Christians. We know of several volumes of writings that date from the first hundred years after Christ, which include, for example, the writings of the third successor of Peter, St. Clement, who wrote an important letter to the church in Corinth settling disputes; the writings of St. Polycarp, the bishop of Smyrna, considered an ecclesiastical writer; the writings of St. Irenaeus of Lyons, the bishop of Lyons and an early ecclesiastical writer who names the twelve bishops of Rome; and the writings of St. Ignatius of Antioch, the bishop of Antioch in Syria for forty years. Many of these writers, being close in time to Jesus and very familiar with the apostles, do not quote what we know as the Gospels. In much the same way that the word of God is revealed in Scripture, however, they are part of the continuous teaching of the church. They are part of its living memory.

To discount the church's tradition with regard to Mary is, therefore, to deny the memory and the mystery of the mystical yet real Body of Christ, alive in the communion of its members for centuries. As Jesus said of this mystical union that would survive from millennium to millennium:

> I do not pray for them alone.
> I pray also for those who will believe in me
> through their word,
> that all may be one
> as you, Father, are in me, and I in you;
> I pray that they may be [one] in us,
> that the world may believe that you sent me. . . .
> that they may be one, as we are one—
> I living in them, you living in me—
> that their unity may be complete.
> So shall the world know that you sent me,
> and that you loved them as you loved me.
> (John 17:20–23)

To be one in Jesus, as he and the Father are one, is the gift Christ gives to the body of believers. But it is also the fountain of our identity as followers of Jesus. This living tradition that we call the church is both fed and defined by Jesus' words, his prayer, that "they may be one" so that the world will come to know not only God's Son through this relationship, but also the fullness of God's love for God's people.

> To discount the church's tradition with regard to Mary is to deny
> the memory and the mystery of the mystical yet real Body of Christ,
> alive in the communion of its members for centuries.

Ecumenical Councils

Both the stories that never became part of the New Testament
proper and the books that eventually became part of the Bible
had a profound and enduring influence on popular opinion
and belief, if not directly on church doctrine. While the New
Testament as we know it is composed of twenty-seven
canonical (judged to be divinely inspired) books, in the first
three and a half centuries of Christianity its contents were still
open to debate. As Peg Streep, author of *Mary, Queen of
Heaven*, notes, "By 190 A.D., twenty of the books, including the
Gospels, were already part of the canon. Arguments over
the inclusion of the additional seven books now in the New
Testament (one of which, the prophetic book of Revelation,
would be very important to the story of Mary) and the
exclusion of others ultimately rejected would not be finally
resolved until 367 A.D." (12).

As early as the second century, bishops got together in
regional meetings, called synods or councils, to take common
action for the doctrinal and pastoral good of their communities
of faithful. These councils have played a highly significant role
in the history of the church by defining truths of revelation as

well as promoting measures of reform or renewal for the church. It was at these gatherings that the church outlined and described issues of faith, morals, worship, and discipline. Ecumenical councils had their model in the Council of Jerusalem—described in chapter 15 of the Acts of the Apostles—which took place in the year 51. At this original gathering, the apostles, under the leadership of Peter, decided that converts to the Christian faith were not obligated to observe all the rules and ordinances of Old Testament law, namely, those concerning circumcision and dietary regulations.

At these early ecumenical councils, the assembled church also produced a common rule of faith, a creed, to be accepted by all the churches in all the cities. Creeds are formal and official statements of religious doctrine—summaries of the principal truths of faith—used for instructional purposes and for actual profession, as well as for the expression of the faith in the liturgy. We know from church history that, from the beginning, the various proposed creeds included statements that proclaimed Jesus as being born of the Holy Spirit and the Virgin Mary, attesting to the fact that Jesus was conceived in the womb of Mary, a virgin, solely by the power of the Holy Spirit. This statement is significant because through it, early believers affirmed that Jesus was conceived by the Holy Spirit, without human seed.

Around the year 100, the Apostles' Creed, not of apostolic origin but reflecting the teaching of the apostles, developed as a formula of faith to be professed by catechumens before the reception of baptism. The acceptance of the truths expressed in this early creed was considered essential for entrance into the church, and included in these truths is the following statement: "I believe . . . in Jesus Christ, his only Son, our Lord; who was conceived by the Holy Spirit, born of the Virgin Mary." By the second century, Irenaeus, a Greek theologian and church father, and later a saint, had already christened Mary with the titles "second Eve" and "intercessor." "In the first 150 years of the history of the church we find that interest in Mary is quite widespread," notes theologian Jim McManus, C.Ss.R., in his book *All Generations Will Call Me Blessed.*

> A bishop like St. Ignatius appealed to Mary's virginal conception to defend the humanity of Jesus; a philosopher like Justin highlighted the parallel between Mary and Eve; the bishop St. Iranaeus from the East brought his interest in Mary to the West and developed his theology of "recapitulation," in which Christ is presented as the new Adam and Mary the new Eve. . . . All the while the Christian faith was spreading throughout the pagan Roman Empire. (45)

During the fourth century, a priest by the name of Arius began to question and eventually deny Jesus' divinity. A creed much more sophisticated than the Apostles' Creed, known as the Nicene Creed, was adopted by the church, largely as a response to the Arian heresy. This creed, still said every Sunday at Mass, declares:

We believe in one Lord, Jesus Christ,
the only Son of God,
eternally begotten of the Father,
God from God, Light from Light,
true God from true God,
begotten, not made, one in Being with the Father. . . .
[B]y the power of the Holy Spirit
he was born of the Virgin Mary, and became man.

This statement of faith proclaims the mystery of the Incarnation: Jesus Christ, the Son of God, is fully divine and also fully human. And Mary, the Blessed Virgin, was placed at the heart of this truth. Since the fifth century, the Nicene Creed has been the only creed in liturgical use in the Eastern churches. The Western church adopted it for liturgical use by the end of the eighth century.

The Council of Ephesus, the third ecumenical council in the history of the Christian church, took place in the year 431, one year after the death of St. Augustine and one year before St. Patrick arrived in Ireland. This council marked a significant moment in the church's understanding of Mary.

It was at this early gathering that the church responded to a growing devotion by assigning to Mary the title of *Theotokos,* meaning "bearer of God," mother of the Son of God made man. As has been true throughout history in the church's relationship with Mary, by defining Mary as the mother of God, the Council of Ephesus proclaimed a fundamental statement about her Son, Jesus the Christ, declaring him the Son of God. The title "mother of God" had already been commonly used by many, including the influential Alexandrian church theologian Origen. "Mary, Mother of God, we salute you," proclaimed St. Cyril of Alexandria (c. 376–444), archbishop of Alexandria in Egypt, at a homily delivered at the Council of Ephesus that is still found in the Office of Readings. "Precious vessel, worthy of the whole world's reverence, you are an ever-shining light, the crown of virginity, the symbol of orthodoxy, an indestructible temple, the place that held him whom no place can contain, mother and virgin. Because of you the holy gospels could say: Blessed is he who comes in the name of the Lord." Both mother and virgin, as human as we are, Mary was yet the sole vessel of God's own Son. It is no wonder that Mary seems both miracle and mystery. Yet in our evolving understanding of Mary, one thing has consistently remained true. As with her life, our theology of Mary has always intended to lead us to a greater understanding of her Son, Jesus. Mary gave birth to Jesus and is, thus, the mother of God, *Theotokos*. So to say that we believe that Mary is the mother of God is to proclaim that Jesus is both the Son of God and one with his Father in the Trinity.

Just as Jesus did not become God in the year 325 at the Council of Nicaea when the church defined his divinity, Mary did not become mother of God at the Council of Ephesus in 431 when the church gave her the official title of *Theotokos*.

MARY IN HISTORY

That was the moment when the Church, in the process of developing and making explicit her faith under the pressure of heresy, became fully aware of this truth and defended it. It's like what happens when a new star is discovered: it is not born when its light first reaches the earth and is observed by someone. It had probably existed for thousands of years. A council definition is the moment in which the light is placed on the candelabrum, which is the creed of the Church. (Cantalamessa, 58)

It was after the Council of Ephesus that the early church's reverence toward Mary rapidly grew. In the century that followed,

Mary would be enthroned in mosaic as Maria Regina ("Mary Queen") in Santa Maria Maggiore in Rome; the first of her feast days would be celebrated. Sometime around 428, Proclus would, in a sermon, call her "the spotless treasure house of virginity, the spiritual paradise of the second; the worship in which two natures were welded together, the one bridge between God and men." (Streep, 84–85)

By the Second Council of Constantinople (553), the doctrine of Mary's perpetual virginity was in place in the faith of the Christian community, leading the ecumenical gathering to use the phrase "ever virgin" (from the Greek *aeiparthenos*) in reference to her.

The last council regarded as ecumenical by Orthodox churches was the Second Council of Nicaea (787), attended by approximately three hundred bishops. This council made a critical distinction in language by defining *adoration* (*latria*) as prayer directed to God alone and *veneration* (*dulia*) as prayer to the saints. Although all prayer is ultimately directed to God, the Christian tradition, even at this early period, saw a natural development in praying to Mary and the saints, asking for their intercession. Just as we seek prayerful intercession from the earthly body of Christ, the early church recognized that we could seek intercession from Christian believers who had died and were regarded as already with God.

Mary's Immaculate Conception

When I was barely eight years old, I received my first Holy Communion on December 8, the feast of the Immaculate Conception, which was also the name of the all-girls school run by Spanish nuns that I attended at the time. Although it often sounds like very complicated theology, the idea of celebrating Mary's singular role in God's plan of salvation by declaring her free from sin from the moment of her conception made sense to me as a child. Even before I understood how babies were conceived, and before I embraced the full impact of a virgin birth at Christmas, I knew that the mother of Jesus must have had a unique and sacred beginning. Long before I grappled with the concept of original sin as an adult, I could understand that Mary, who gave birth to the Son of God, must have lived in an entirely unique and holy grace from the beginning. Some ideas simply make more sense when we are children hearing through our hearts than when we are adults analyzing them as concepts in our minds. Or as Jesus reminds us: "Trust me when I tell you that whoever does not accept the kingdom of God as a child will not enter into it" (Luke 18:17).

The Christian church proclaimed that Mary was conceived in the womb of her mother without the sin of our human race, without original sin. She was pure at her conception. In a unique and special way, Mary was "full of grace" from the very beginning, protected from the consequences of original sin that every other human inherits.

> The Fathers of the Eastern tradition call the Mother of God "the All-Holy" (Panagia) and celebrate her as "free from any stain of sin, as though fashioned by the Holy Spirit and formed as a new creature." By the grace of God Mary remained free of every personal sin her whole life long. (Catechism, 493)

Although it was a widely held belief long before then, this great revealed truth was not confirmed until December 8,

1854, when Mary's Immaculate Conception was declared a dogma—a true doctrine of faith—of the church by Pius IX. According to historians, the feast of the conception of the mother of God was celebrated as early as the eighth century in Palestine, Constantinople, and other parts of the East. It was imported into Italy and Ireland as an actual feast day by the ninth century, and subsequently throughout the rest of Europe. Mary's conception was set on December 8, exactly nine months before her celebrated birthday, September 8.

In the papal bull *Ineffabilis Deus,* Pope Pius IX declared: "The most Blessed Virgin Mary was, from the first moment of her conception, by a singular grace and privilege of almighty God and by virtue of the merits of Jesus Christ, Savior of the human race, preserved immune from all stain of original sin." In other words, in order to become the mother of the Savior, Mary was enriched with gifts and graces appropriate to such a role and purpose, including being redeemed from original sin from the moment of her own conception, a grace not shared with any other human. It is indisputable that God blessed Mary in a distinct way by choosing her to give birth to his Son. The dogma of the Immaculate Conception acknowledges that Mary was granted unique grace from the moment of her conception because of the merits of her Son.

Mary's Birth and Presentation

In addition to the early artistic representations of Mary and her life, the mother of Jesus and her parents were also mentioned in apocryphal literature, early Christian writings proposed as additions to the New Testament but rejected officially by the major canons. Some of these writings or statements, while sometimes considered to be of questionable authorship or authenticity, are regarded by some as eyewitness accounts. It is in the Protevangelium of James, for example, recognized as an unhistorical account, that we read of Mary's birth and of Mary's parents, Anne and Joachim, who offered their daughter to God in the temple when she was three years old in order to carry out a promise made to God when Anne was still childless.

According to extrabiblical sources dating back to the second century, Mary of Nazareth was born to Anne and Joachim, who, like Abraham and Sarah, prayed to God hoping for a child. Neither Joachim nor Anne (Ann, or Anna) are mentioned in the Scriptures, although St. Anne's life was first described in early apocryphal writings. The Protevangelium of James and Jacobus de Voragine's thirteenth-century lives of the saints, *The Golden Legend*, tell the story of an angel who appeared to St. Anne and told her that their prayers would be answered and that she would bear a child, a very graced child.

Evidence of formal devotion to St. Anne is found in sixth-century documents in the East, and by the tenth century it was widespread in the West. The Western church celebrates the feast of Mary's parents, her first teachers in the ways of faith, on July 26.

Nothing is written in the canonical Scriptures about Mary's life before the Annunciation. Early extrabiblical accounts, however, say that Mary was greeted by the high priest Zechariah as Anne and Joachim presented her in the temple. Though not a biblical account, Mary's presentation—first celebrated as a feast in the sixth century in Jerusalem and still celebrated on November 21—has an important theological purpose in its bearing on the feasts of the Immaculate Conception and of the birth of Mary. In the same way that the Immaculate Conception emphasizes Mary's holiness from the beginning of her life, the feast of her presentation points to her parents' continued devotion and dedication to God through her early childhood and beyond. Mary the young child, Mary the young woman, grew to become a worthy temple of the Holy Spirit.

Other ancient traditions indicate that Mary was taught by the prophetess Anna, to whom she was presented early in life. Whatever the actual details of her life, it is not difficult to imagine Anne and Joachim's gratitude for their daughter, and the dedication with which they shared their faith tradition with Mary. The childhood of Mary was, no doubt, that of a typical Jewish girl of her time. Working through her parents, the Holy Spirit taught Mary the ways of prayer and generosity. She learned the Scriptures and listened to the prophets' call for a holy people. She learned to love God and to discern his will even in the smallest events. As were all Jews, surely Mary was eager for the coming of the Messiah and the deliverance that God would bring to the people of Israel. "The Word of God, incorporeal, incorruptible and immaterial, entered our world," declared saint and bishop Athanasius in a treatise written around 318 entitled *On the Incarnation.* "Within the Virgin he built himself a temple, that is, a body; he made it his own instrument in which to dwell and to reveal himself. In this way he received from mankind a body like our own, and, since all were subject to the corruption of death, he delivered this body over to death for all, and with supreme love offered it to the Father."

Much of what we "know" about Mary combines different written and oral traditions to create a story that brings to life this woman and her role in our salvation history. Even though I grew up with my grandfather and lived under the same roof with him for many years, when he died three years ago, I discovered details of his childhood and stories of his life that I had never known before. This is part of a family's living tradition, and in some ways, it is always evolving. In the same way, the body of Christian believers shared stories with each other about Jesus' mother, many of which we now know as "tradition," even if they are not directly attributed to a biblical source.

Mary's Assumption

Because of her unique role as the mother of God, the Feast of the Assumption celebrates Mary's being taken up body and soul into heaven, thus entering eternity in completeness at the end of her life on earth. Some of the earliest traditions of the church in the East celebrated the falling asleep of the Virgin, as it is still known in Byzantine rite. The assumption of Mary is one of the oldest and most solemn feasts, with a history dating back to at least the seventh century, when the feast was already established in Jerusalem and Rome as the Dormition of Mary. This statement is first found in New Testament apocryphal writings dating from the fourth century.

The text of the Byzantine Liturgy for the Feast of Dormition notes, "In giving birth you kept your virginity; in your Dormition you did not leave the world, O Mother of God, but were joined to the source of Life. You conceived the living God and, by your prayers, will deliver our souls from death." This truth of faith was based on several details noted about Mary from the earliest records—the biblical words of the angel Gabriel at the Annunciation about Mary's holiness, her continuing faithful witness of the cross, and later symbols that imagined her as the church in the book of Revelation: "A great sign appeared in the sky, a woman clothed with the sun, with the moon under her feet, and on her head a crown of twelve stars" (12:1). According to tradition, the house where

Mary was said to have died in the company of the remaining apostles existed and was preserved into the fourth century.

During the Middle Ages, Christian piety proclaimed belief in the assumption of Mary into heaven in the fourth glorious mystery of the holy rosary, pointing again to Revelation 12:1. But it was only on November 1, 1950, that Pope Pius XII, after consultation with the bishops, proclaimed the assumption of Mary as a dogma of faith of the Catholic Church, stating that "the Immaculate Mother of God, ever-Virgin Mary, on the completion of the course of her earthly life, has been taken up, in body and soul, to the glory of heaven" (Bettenson, 281). The Western church celebrates this holy event as the assumption of Mary on August 15.

The assumption of Mary has been described as "the fitting fulfillment of the Immaculate Conception." Indeed, this tradition and dogma builds on the groundwork of faith already laid and defined by the Immaculate Conception. The only person to be fully human yet conceived without original sin, Mary is granted a final singular grace and privilege—to participate in her own Son's resurrection by being taken into heaven, body and soul, at the end of her life. Mary, the first Christian, the first to follow Jesus the Christ, is also the first to experience with him the fullness of eternity.

For the rest of us who profess weekly in the creed that we "look for the resurrection of the dead, and the life of the world to come," Mary's assumption gives us hope and reminds us of our own salvific end. On the last day, we look forward, as Mary did, to a new, incorruptible spiritual self, united in both body and soul. As St. Paul says in his first letter to the Corinthians:

> The trumpet will sound and the dead will be raised incorruptible, and we shall be changed. This corruptible body must be clothed with incorruptibility, this mortal body with immortality.... [T]hen will the saying of Scripture be fulfilled: ... "O death, where is your victory? O death, where is your sting?"... [T]hanks be to God who has given us the victory through our Lord Jesus Christ. (15:52–55, 57)

Queen of Heaven

Another traditional belief emphasizing Mary's role in the drama of salvation and in the life of the church is that of Mary as Queen of Heaven, a feast inaugurated on August 22, 1954, by Pope Pius XII. Not only was the Immaculate Virgin preserved free from all guilt of original sin and taken up body and soul into heavenly glory, the pope declared, but she was also "exalted by the Lord as Queen over all things, so that she might be the more fully conformed to her Son, the Lord of lords and conqueror of sin and death." Because of Mary's participation in the victory of her Son on the cross, Jesus crowns her queen of all nations and peoples.

Although identifying Mary as Queen of Heaven might have meant more in a different culture or in a different era of monarchs and other royalty, celebrating Mary as queen is a natural and straightforward feast. As the mother of the one who is King of kings, Mary will forever hold a unique and distinguished place in our faith history. Because of her Son, she is queen over all creation.

Mary, the New Eve

Referring to Mary as the "new Eve" is one of the most ancient traditions, dating back to as early as the second century and developed mostly by St. Justin Martyr (d. c. 165) and St. Irenaeus (d. c. 202). Both of these fathers of the church saw a parallel between the obedience of Mary and the disobedience of Eve, much in the same way that Paul in his letter to the Romans drew a parallel between Adam and Jesus, saying: "Just as a single offense brought condemnation to all men, a single righteous act brought all men acquittal and life. Just as through one man's disobedience all became sinners, so through one man's obedience all shall become just" (Romans 5:18–19).

As St. Justin Martyr explained, "Eve, when she was still a virgin, accepted the serpent's word and gave birth to disobedience and death. Instead, Mary, the Virgin, accepting with faith and joy the good news given by the angel Gabriel, answered: 'Let it be done to me according to your word.'" And St. Irenaeus declared: "That which Eve had bound through her unbelief, Mary loosened through her faith." In this way, because she is the mother of the "new Adam," Mary is called the "new Eve," the mother of all the living.

Mary as Intercessor

Asking Mary, our heavenly and spiritual mother given to us by Jesus at the Crucifixion, to pray for us is nothing more than asking for her intercession on our behalf. It is a natural and very human role. When we are in need, when we want to especially thank God for our blessings, we ask our friends and family to pray for us. In light of this, what is more natural than turning to the woman who gave birth to Jesus and asking her to pray with us and for us in spite of our weakness and sinfulness?

We pray with and through Mary and the saints, asking that they intercede with God on our behalf. Without a doubt, this can easily become a vague theological concept unless we are able to place it within a human context, a human understanding. Several years ago, I was given the opportunity to experience exactly that—a powerful human image of motherly intercession.

In the spring of 1993, I attended a prayer service led by Detroit's auxiliary bishop, Thomas Gumbleton, who was visiting Austin, Texas, as a participant in a statewide conference. Held across the street from the stately governor's mansion, the prayer service was part of a sustained vigil on behalf of Irineo Tristán Montoya, a twenty-six year old convicted in Texas of murder and sentenced to death by lethal injection. It was here that I met Emilia Tristán. Emilia had been camping with her husband in a makeshift shelter under the trees across the street from the mansion for several weeks, requesting the opportunity to meet with then-Texas governor Ann Richards face-to-face, mother-to-mother, even if for a mere few minutes. Emilia had traveled thousands of miles from their native Tampico, Mexico, seeking to speak to someone in authority on her son's behalf.

As days turned into weeks, Emilia and her supporters fasted, held daily prayer services, and whenever possible, received the Eucharist as they waited patiently, zealously, persistently. To anyone who would listen, Emilia told the story of her son, who was only eighteen years old at the time of the crime. The fact that her son, a Spanish speaker, had signed an English confession without a lawyer present resulted in many legal questions. But it was his mother's perseverance and passion as she pleaded for mercy for her son that has been ingrained in my memory. "For eight years I have not been able to touch my son, but only look at him across a glass wall," Emilia said. "I want to hold him against my chest and hug him."

In a very real way, this mother did everything within her human power to intercede on behalf of her condemned son. And the church, through Bishop Gumbleton, joined her as he interceded with the civil authorities on her behalf. Emilia Tristán showed me that even when our actions state that we don't deserve mercy, the unconditional love of a mother leads her to plead continually for a merciful resolution. While our minds may not understand fully the theology of intercession, our hearts can easily grasp the love that empowers parents such as Emilia to intercede on their children's behalf. Without a doubt, this image of a human mother's persistent intercession is a powerful reminder of the unconditional and merciful love that awaits me when I seek my heavenly mother's intercession.

While our minds may not understand fully the theology of intercession, our hearts can easily grasp the love that empowers parents to intercede on their children's behalf.

Holy Mary, Mother of God, Pray for Us!

The miracle at the wedding in Cana was the first time Mary interceded before her Son on behalf of someone in need. Pope John Paul II, in his encyclical letter *Mother of the Redeemer,* explains the story in this way: "The description of the Cana event outlines what is actually manifested as a new kind of motherhood according to the spirit and not just according to the flesh, that is to say, Mary's solicitude for human beings, her concern for them in their wants and needs." As a guest at the wedding feast, Mary noted the possible embarrassment of the newly married couple and their families. Her role, as mother of Jesus and intercessor for the church, is to show her maternal compassion on behalf of the world's needs.

Christ is the mediator between God and human beings, and Mary is the mediatrix between Christ and us. As Archbishop Sheen notes of the miracle at Cana, Mary intercedes to gain for us what we need, without our always knowing our needs.

> Neither the wine stewards nor the diners knew that the wine was failing; therefore, they could not ask for help. In like manner, if we do not know what our soul needs, how can we put such needs in our prayers? Often we do not know what is vital to our lives. . . . That is where devotion to Mary comes in. The people at the table did not know what they needed to maintain the joy of the marriage feast, even when the Lord was in their midst. There are many of us who would not come to Our Lord unless we had someone who knows our needs better than we know ourselves and who will ask Our Lord for us. This role of Mary makes her acceptable to everyone. (116–17)

The history of the Catholic Church is above all a story of a people of faith. From the first recorded stories of the early Christians, difficult situations and events in history are interwoven with stories of how people lived out their faith. In Acts and in the letters of Paul, we find numerous examples of Christians living out—and sometimes dying for—the message of Christ that is recorded in the Gospels.

Chapter 7 of Acts records the death of Stephen, a deacon who was stoned to death at Jerusalem and who is venerated as the first Christian martyr. It also describes the death of James the Greater, who was beheaded in the year 44, the first apostle to die. We hear about Phillip's journey to Samaria, his performing miracles and proclaiming the Messiah. "There were many who had unclean spirits, which came out shrieking loudly. Many others were paralytics or cripples, and these were cured. The rejoicing in that town rose to fever pitch" (Acts 8:7–8). It is the authenticity of these lives, of their way of living the gospel, that speaks to us as a church. Their lives speak louder than any idea or doctrine. Their example, their lives of spirit and action, brings the doctrine of our faith to life.

It was, therefore, natural for the church to record and preserve stories of the lives of other individuals, holy persons throughout the centuries who died and are believed to be in glory with God in heaven. These holy people are called saints. The veneration of saints evolved out of the faith of the early Christian church as a way of honoring those who had lived out the gospel message in a real and authentic way. Believers also requested their intercession with God. As Franciscan Fr. Richard Rohr points out:

> The saints of every age have revealed the truth of Jesus to that age. . . . Because of their openness to God they were mediators of grace and they radiated that grace to

the world around them. In the lives of the saints we can discern how God works in human life.... Although each of the saints had their own particular way of viewing and living the gospel, all of them were unbiased in the sense that they put their selfish concerns aside and opened themselves radically to the truth that God was speaking to them. They were in as total union with God as it is humanly possible to be. They threw themselves completely into doing not what they wanted but what God wanted. They surrendered themselves wholly, which is what made them holy. (114)

In much the same way that they realized the need to acknowledge saints in their midst, the early Christian church naturally recognized Mary's unique role in the mystery of Christ and honored her with special reverence. And as early Christians faced abominable and continuous persecution, they turned to Mary, the mother of their Savior, to intercede for them.

St. Athanasius (c. 297–373), the archbishop of Alexandria, wrote:

It is becoming to you to be mindful of us as you stand near him who granted you all graces, for you are the Mother of God, Queen, Lady and Mistress. Do so for the King, the Lord God and Master who was born of you. For this reason you are called "full of grace."

Remember us, most holy Virgin, and bestow on us gifts from the riches of your graces, O Virgin full of grace. Amen. (Dollen, 35)

And St. Ephraem the Deacon (306–73), born in what is now Syria, prayed:

O Virgin Immaculate, Mother of God and my Mother, from your sublime heights turn your eyes of pity upon me. Filled with confidence in your goodness and knowing full well your power, I beg you to extend to me your assistance in the journey of life, which is so full of dangers for my soul. In order that I may never be a slave of the devil through sin but may ever live with my heart humble and pure, I entrust myself wholly to you. I consecrate my heart to you forever, my only desire being to love your divine Son, Jesus. Mary, none of your devout servants has ever perished; may I, too, be saved. Amen. (Dollen, 36)

For early Christians, addressing Mary of Nazareth, the mother of their Savior, as their own spiritual mother was a natural and authentic occurrence. It simply made sense. Yet as time goes on and as decades turn into centuries and now into millennia, being able to explain this relationship within the context of a shared faith is often a question of doctrine rather than an instance of kinship, as it once was.

Ad summum Regina thronum
                    defertur in altum:
Angelicis praelata choris,
cui festus et ipse Filius occurrens
Matrem super aethera ponit.

The Queen is borne to the highest throne on high:
preceded by angelic chorus
the rejoicing Son himself coming to meet her
establishes his mother above the skies.

—Inscription identifying a sculpture of the coronation of the Virgin
on Martin Luther's burial chamber in the Castle Church in
Wittenberg, on whose door he had posted his infamous Ninety-five
Theses (Stravinskas, 73; translation by Charles H. Miller, S.M.)

CHAPTER FOUR

Mary in Other Faith Traditions

Mother of God, Mother of All

In an unfortunate paradox caused by our human frailty, Mary, our common mother in Christ, has become a source of division among Christians, often widening the gap between Catholics and Protestants. Many Protestants mistake Marian devotion for adoration. Some accuse Catholics of making her a goddess. Others question the teaching on perpetual virginity; after all, they point out, Scripture refers to Christ's brothers. My husband, Michael, even had a university student years ago who argued that the Catholic Mary was the "whore of Babylon." Less extreme, but no less inaccurate, are those who think the Catholic Church gives Mary a status equal to that of her Son.

A good place to start to solve this puzzle is with the Nativity story. One of my favorite Christmas traditions is one that I inherited from my grandfather Alipio Páez. Every year of his adult life until his death at the age of ninety-five, Alipio set up a Nativity scene that could easily compete with the elaborate displays put on by many chain department stores. Not satisfied with presenting just the figurines of Mary, Joseph, Jesus, and the rest of the usual characters, Alipio would carefully build an entire town of Bethlehem, Caribbean style, with plenty of palm trees, rivers, tall blooming trees, papier-mâché mountains painted in shades of green and brown, and even plastic pigs to keep the miniature sheep and their shepherds company. Alipio's Bethlehem centered on the glorious crèche. Every year a new piece, a new scene, would add flavor to his detailed handmade miniature Nativity setting.

In bringing his own world to Bethlehem, Alipio was not saying that the biblical details of the Christmas story were unimportant to him. It was rather the opposite. By bringing to life the environment of the story beyond the *pesebre,* the humble crèche, my grandfather emphasized the central truth—the actual point—of the story! God loved his people so much that he was born of a woman to be one with us. She gave birth to a baby who was the Son of God. In that humble stable, the mystery and wonder of the Incarnation came to life. The virgin birth. The Son of God conceived in the womb of Mary. A baby in Mary's arms, both true God and true man. The deepest and most complicated elements of Christian theology are incarnated in the crèche.

Certainly we can all agree that Mary was crucially instrumental in Jesus' birth. It is in the fact and the meaning of Mary's motherhood that all Christians can begin to come together. This definitive start, this shared reality is the reason why Christians in the early centuries found it natural and fitting to address Mary as *Theotokos*. If the meaning of the Nativity is to be taken seriously, calling Mary by the title "mother of God" should be nothing less than the natural meeting point for all Christians. It is also the oldest and most important title assigned to the mother of Jesus—and the only ecumenical title assigned to her—for it was defined in 431 by the early Christian church as a truth of faith to be believed by all.

Although Scripture never calls Mary the mother of God, the Gospel tells us that she conceived and gave birth to a son, "called Son of the Most High. . . . Son of God" (Luke 1:32, 35). This modest maiden who "found favor with God" was recognized by Elizabeth simply as "the mother of my Lord" (Luke 1:43). To believe that Jesus is both man and God, to proclaim that he is Son of God, is to acknowledge that Mary is the mother of our Lord, the mother of God. The title "mother of God" directly attests to the fact that Jesus is God—fully human and fully divine. "That anyone could doubt the right of the holy Virgin to be called the Mother of God fills me with astonishment. Surely she must be the Mother of God if our Lord Jesus Christ is God, and she gave birth to him!" exclaimed St. Cyril of Alexandria, a theologian and bishop from the late 300s and early 400s, in a letter now found in the Office of Readings. "Our Lord's disciples may not have used those exact words," he pointed out, "but they delivered to us the belief those words enshrine, and this has also been taught us by the holy fathers." As John of Damascus declared two hundred years later, "This name contains the whole mystery of the Incarnation."

The denial that Mary had God in her womb is actually an early Christian heresy known as Nestorianism (condemned since the 400s), which claims that Jesus was a human person joined to the divine person of God's Son. Protestant Bible scholars and reformers alike have rejected the Nestorian heresy, acknowledging that Jesus is one person, but with two natures, making him fully divine and fully human.

> The unique and altogether singular event of the Incarnation of the Son of God does not mean that Jesus Christ is part God and part man, nor does it imply that he is the result of a confused mixture of the divine and the human. He became truly man while remaining truly God. Jesus Christ is true God and true man. (Catechism, 464)

There is a lot we don't know about the historical Mary, and so, like Alipio with his Bethlehem scene, we speculate about it and fill in the gaps with the material of our own lives. But there is no doubt that Mary remains central to the truth of God's salvation history. This historic woman embodies our common Christian faith: the Son of God was also the Son of Mary, a real and very human woman. And everything that we know or proclaim about the mother of Jesus is meant to call attention to her Son. Mary leads us to him who is the way, the truth, and the life. Indeed, from the beginning of the Christian church, believers have honored Mary because God chose this woman to have a special place in our history of salvation. Never before or since has God become flesh in a woman in order to dwell among us. If we accept Jesus Christ as the Son of God, then we must honor Jesus' mother as unique and favored—or in the words of the angel Gabriel, as "blessed" among all men and women.

Archbishop Fulton J. Sheen used the image of the sun and the moon to describe the intense relationship that God created between Mary and her spiritual children.

> God, who made the sun, also made the moon. The moon does not take away from the brilliance of the sun. The moon would be only a burnt-out cinder floating in the immensity of space were it not for the sun. All its light is reflected from the sun. The Blessed Mother reflects her Divine Son; without Him, she is nothing. With Him, she is the Mother of Men. On dark nights we are grateful for the moon; when we see it shining, we know there must be a sun. So in this dark night of the world when men turn their backs on Him who is the Light of the World, we look to Mary to

guide their feet while we await the sunrise. (Sheen, 76–77)

What a beautiful image for Mary, whose entire life not only reflected but, indeed, projected the light of her Son for the whole world to see.

It is in the fact and the meaning of Mary's motherhood that all Christians can begin to come together.

Early Protestants and Mary

It is interesting to note that the first Protestant Reformers did not oppose or challenge the church's devotion to the Virgin Mary. Such attacks, points out Catholic apologist and writer Fr. Peter M. J. Stravinskas, came from their successors. Marian doctrines, in fact, were taken for granted and accepted by sixteenth-century Protestant Reformers. Stravinskas quotes Thomas O'Meara's *Mary in Protestant and Catholic Theology:*

It was the times with their changes in intellectual and cultural outlook, it was the very history of the Reform with its forgetfulness of the fullness of its Lutheran and Calvinist inheritance, which caused a Christian religion to come into existence without any place for Christ's Mother. We should remember that this was

MARY IN OTHER FAITH TRADITIONS

not the view of the Reformers, nor is it intrinsic to
Protestantism. (Stravinskas, 79)

According to historians, the original Protestant Reformers
were actually in agreement over much of what is now
considered divisive Marian theology. These Reformers took
Mary and her place in the church seriously, not challenging
Catholic Mariology except when it came to devotional
practices. The teachings of the Reformers continued to affirm
the virginal conception and the divine maternity, as well as
the perpetual virginity of Mary. While striving to terminate
or reform what they saw as excesses of the medieval church
in the piety or devotional practices regarding Mary, the
original Reformers remained in agreement regarding Mary's
perpetual virginity and her unique and honored role in the
Christian faith.

Martin Luther spoke of Mary's humility, which allowed
God's plan to be carried out through her. "In this work
whereby she was made the Mother of God, so many and such
good things were given her that no one can grasp them,"
Luther said. "Not only was Mary the mother of Him who is
born [in Bethlehem], but of Him who, before the world, was
eternally born of the Father from a Mother in time and at the
same time man and God." He defended the virginity of Mary
as part of the mystery of Christ's coming into the world. "It is
an article of faith that Mary is Mother of the Lord and still a

virgin," Luther wrote. "Christ, we believe, came forth from a womb left perfectly intact."

Ulrich Zwingli, founder of the Reformation in Switzerland, also affirmed the doctrine of Mary as mother of God, saying, "It was given to her what belongs to no creature, that in the flesh she should bring forth the Son of God." And he defended the doctrine of Mary's perpetual virginity: "I firmly believe that Mary, according to the words of the gospel as a pure Virgin brought forth for us the Son of God and in childbirth and after childbirth forever remained a pure, intact Virgin." Zwingli even stressed, "The more the honor and love of Christ increases among men, so much the esteem and honor given to Mary should grow."

John Calvin's approach to Mariology is a bit more radical than Luther's. He "appears to have accepted all the traditional Marian doctrines, including the as-yet-undefined teachings on the Immaculate Conception and Assumption," notes Stravinskas, "but in its main lines, is not much different, although he senses a greater urgency to hem it in with more qualifications" (110). Indeed, although Calvin was not as lavish as Luther in his praise of Mary, he didn't deny her perpetual virginity, often referring to Mary as "Holy Virgin." Calvin also held that Mary was the Mother of God.

In Calvin's own words:

> It cannot be denied that God in choosing and destining Mary to be the Mother of his Son, granted

her the highest honor.... Elizabeth called Mary Mother of the Lord, because the unity of the person in the two natures of Christ was such that she could have said that the mortal man engendered in the womb of Mary was at the same time the eternal God.

As Stravinskas points out:

It seems that, often enough, Calvin went to particular lengths to assert that "Calvinists are not foes of Mary, but they feel that they have given her true honor, whereas others have taken from God and given to Mary. Throughout Calvin's sermons on the Scriptures, there are occasional references to the dishonor rendered to Mary and to God by her various titles and by Roman theology." (Stravinskas, 76)

Over the following centuries, however, the polemics of the post-Reformation period generated, at best, a deep silence regarding Mary. On the one hand, the Virgin Mary became the sign of Catholic orthodoxy. And on the other hand, the evolving and expanding Protestant branches developed a strict and absolutist understanding of revelation as stemming from Scripture alone, *sola Scriptura*, making Marian doctrine inadmissible, since much of it can't be directly found in the Bible. By contrast with historic Reformation Protestantism, Stravinskas points out, classical fundamentalism "admits no role for Mary," although a few

MARY IN OTHER FAITH TRADITIONS

contemporary fundamentalist theologians indicate a "willingness to reflect on some possible position for the Mother of Jesus in Christian spirituality, within biblical limitations as they prescribe them" (212).

Everything that we know or proclaim about the mother of Jesus is meant to call attention to her Son.

Mary, Our Mother, Intercede for Us

Perhaps for non-Catholics, the most problematic role that Catholics give to Mary is that of mediator, or intercessor. Some think that the request voiced in the final line of the Hail Mary—"pray for us sinners, now and at the hour of our death"—denies outright the biblical teaching found in 1 Timothy 2:5–6: "And the truth is this: 'God is one. One also is the mediator between God and men, the man Christ Jesus, who gave himself as a ransom for all.'" But praying on behalf of one another cannot interfere with Christ's mediating role. In the verses preceding the quote from this pastoral letter, Paul also instructs Christians to pray for each other: "I urge that petitions, prayers, intercessions, and thanksgivings be offered for all men. . . . Prayer of this kind is good, and God our savior is pleased with it" (1 Timothy 2:1, 3). The New Testament, in fact, offers plenty of suggestions that the faithful pray for one another:

MARY IN OTHER FAITH TRADITIONS

I beg you, brothers, for the sake of our Lord Jesus Christ and the love of the Spirit, join me in the struggle by your prayers to God on my behalf. (Romans 15:30)

Is there anyone sick among you? He should ask for the presbyters of the church. They in turn are to pray over him, anointing him with oil in the Name [of the Lord]. This prayer uttered in faith will reclaim the one who is ill, and the Lord will restore him to health. If he has committed any sins, forgiveness will be his. Hence, declare your sins to one another, and pray for one another, that you may find healing.

The fervent petition of a holy man is powerful indeed. (James 5:14–16)

My command to you is: love your enemies, pray for your persecutors. (Matthew 5:44)

At every opportunity pray in the Spirit, using prayers and petitions of every sort. Pray constantly and attentively for all in the holy company. Pray for me that God may put his word on my lips, that I may courageously make known the mystery of the gospel— that mystery for which I am an ambassador in chains.

MARY IN OTHER FAITH TRADITIONS

Pray that I may have courage to proclaim it as I ought. (Ephesians 6:18–20)

The charge that Mary is a comediator is simply a nonissue. Catholic theology stresses that we have but one mediator: Jesus.

Within a rightly ordered faith, asking for Mary's intercession is an expression of our solidarity in the communion of saints that is comparable, in a very real way, to asking other living persons to pray for us, to mediate on our behalf through intercessory prayer. "The maternal duty of Mary toward men in no way obscures or diminishes this unique mediation of Christ, but rather shows its power," noted the documents of the Second Vatican Council. "For all the saving influences of the Blessed Virgin on men . . . flow forth from the superabundance of the merits of Christ, rest on his mediation, depend entirely on it, draw all their power from it." As long as the person praying remains focused on Christ, therefore, asking for prayers from Mary—and other saints—is within the instructions we read in Scripture to "pray in the Spirit" through "intercessions" and "prayers and petitions of every sort."

Catholic theology stresses a broader understanding of mediation that encompasses not only people but also ideas and things. God's creation, for example, can and does lead us to God. In this sense, the sacraments, holy water, sacred oil, and the saints are all like Mary, mediators of grace for us as Christians. All things point us toward the One who created and blessed life in each of us. Because of Mary's obedience, faith, and hope, she cooperated, in a singular and exceptional way, in Jesus' work and ministry of salvation. "Mary gave her consent in faith at the Annunciation and maintained it without hesitation at the foot of the Cross," notes the Catholic Catechism. "Ever since, her motherhood has extended to the brothers and sisters of her Son 'who still journey on earth surrounded by dangers and difficulties.' Jesus, the only mediator, is the way of our prayer; Mary, his mother and ours, is wholly transparent to him: she 'shows the way,' and is herself 'the Sign' of the way." We entrust to the mother of Jesus our supplications and praises "because she knows the humanity which, in her, the Son of God espoused" (Catechism, 2674–75). When we ask in prayer for Mary's intercession, we are adhering with her to the plan of the Father. "Like the beloved disciple we welcome Jesus' mother into our homes, for she has become the mother of all the living. We can pray with and to her. The prayer of the Church is sustained by the prayer of Mary and united with it in hope" (Catechism, 2679).

The word *mediation,* from the Latin *mediatus,* not only means to intervene or, specifically, to act as an intermediary. It also suggests the act of promoting reconciliation, of seeking a settlement or compromise. In the Eastern church, the image of Mary as intermediary of God's grace on behalf of unworthy sinners was accepted early on in history. According to the *Encyclopedia of Catholicism,* the idea that

MARY IN OTHER FAITH TRADITIONS

Mary had a maternal influence, that she could turn away Christ's just anger and obtain mercy for sinners, was very common.

This is seen, for example, in the popularity of the Theophilus legend, which was translated into Latin in the eighth century. In this story, a man named Theophilus bargains his soul away to the devil to gain a lucrative job. When he is near death, Theophilus implores Mary to get back the contract, which she does after contending with the devil. Theophilus dies forgiven and avoids eternal hell.

Pope John Paul II reflected in *Redemptoris Mater* on the role of Mary and her presence in the life of the church:

> Mary's mediation is intimately linked with her motherhood. It possesses a specifically maternal character, which distinguishes it from the mediation of the other creatures who in various and always subordinate ways share in the one mediation of Christ, although her own mediation is also a shared mediation. . . . This role is at the same time special and extraordinary. It flows from her divine motherhood and can be understood and lived in faith only on the basis of the full truth of this motherhood.

All Christians, the pope noted, must deepen in themselves and in each of their communities that "obedience of faith" of which Mary "is the first and brightest example."

Christians know that their unity will be truly discovered only if it is based on the unity of their faith. They must resolve considerable discrepancies of doctrine concerning the mystery and ministry of the Church, and sometimes also concerning the role of Mary in the work of salvation. Mary, who is still the model of this pilgrimage, is to lead them to the unity which is willed by their one Lord, and which is so much desired by those who are attentively listening to what "the Spirit is saying to the churches" today.

In this way, rather than being a source of division among Christian faiths, Mary's unique and singular role in the history of our salvation can be an element of our unity. It is her obedience and faithfulness that we honor. It is her example that we emulate. And it is her intercession on our behalf that we seek as we journey on this earth, remaining bound toward eternal life with Christ.

Who Are My Brothers?

He was still addressing the crowds when his mother and his brothers appeared outside to speak with him. Someone said to him, "Your mother and your brothers are standing out there and they wish to speak to you." He said to the one who had told him, "Who is my mother? Who are my brothers?" Then, extending his hand toward his disciples, he said, "There are my mother and my brothers. Whoever does the will of my heavenly Father is brother and sister and mother to me." (Matthew 12:46–50; see also Mark 3:31–35)

The question of whether Mary had children besides Jesus can't be totally settled by Scripture. The passage above is one of about ten instances in the New Testament where "brothers" and "sisters" of the Lord are mentioned, a reference that is often used by non-Catholics to point out that Mary was a virgin only until the birth of Jesus. Most non-Catholics believe that after Jesus was born, Mary and Joseph had other children, whom Scripture refers to as "the brothers of the Lord."

According to Catholic theology, however, Jesus was the only son of Mary and Joseph. And Catholics believe that the Virgin Mary remained a virgin consecrated to God throughout her life. The title *Ever Virgin*, in fact, arose early in Christianity, with the Synod of Milan (A.D. 391) being the first in the West to give a clear rationale for the ever-virgin theology. The phrase *Mary's perpetual virginity* continued to be commonly used in the Middle Ages and was used in Protestant confessional writings among Reformers such as Luther, Calvin, and Zwingli (Brown, et al., *Mary in the New Testament*, 65). To call Mary "Ever Virgin," therefore, is an ancient tradition. It is an important tradition because it honors Mary as a model of what it means to live a holy, pure life dedicated only to God.

Mary's virginity is an integral part of the mystery of the Incarnation and a great privilege—one that she is to enjoy forever. But to understand the essence of the ever-virgin doctrine requires that we comprehend virginity not only in the physical sense, but also in a spiritual one. Called to a singular vocation, Mary gave herself entirely to her Creator, body and soul, therefore belonging only to God. Like religious men and women in modern times who are living a vow of celibacy, Mary's love was deliberate and focused on the perfect love that can come only from God. In this way, Mary's virginity is nothing less than a living sign of the kingdom. As with other aspects of her life, this complete, unqualified yes to God and God alone models for all Christians the undivided heart that God requests of all of us.

Aside from the aspects of this doctrine that have derived from tradition, there are several important points to note in order to understand any biblical references to "brother." First, Jesus is the only child of Mary mentioned in Scripture. Even when the "brethren" of Jesus are mentioned, it is never stated that these kinsmen are children of Mary, as Jesus is. Furthermore, the word *brethren* itself has proven to be problematic. Translated from the Greek *adelphos,* this term for "brother" in the Bible is not restricted to the literal meaning of a full brother or half brother. According to Scripture scholars, it is well known that in the New Testament the word *adelphos* at times indicates other relationships, including that of disciples. Sometimes the word was used to mean kinsmen or relatives as well as brothers and sisters. The same goes for the term for "sister" (*adelphe*) and the plural form for "brothers" (*adelphoi*). The problems arise from the fact that neither Hebrew nor Aramaic, the language spoken by Christ and his disciples, has a word equivalent to *cousin*, so people often used the word *brother* to describe that relationship as well.

In addition to this, the Jewish notion of family, which was very important in their cultural and religious understanding, can be considered parallel to what our current culture refers to as "extended" family. There are some cultural equivalents of this Jewish definition of family even today. In the Hispanic and Asian cultures, for example, the larger family unit—including grandparents, uncles, aunts, cousins, nephews, nieces—is understood as the "family." In other words, no distinction is made between "immediate" and "extended" families. This can be a hard concept to understand for people living in a culture in which the word *family* is often restricted to a limited legal definition of people living in the immediate household. So important to the Jews of Jesus' day was this concept of the extended family, notes Scripture scholar Anthony E. Gilles, "that the Hebrew language had not developed a word for 'cousin,' since one's cousin was thought of as simply another member of the extended family, that is, as a 'brother' or 'sister.' This lack in the Hebrew (and Aramaic) language of a word for 'cousin' was acknowledged by the Greek translators of the Hebrew Old Testament as well as by the writers of the Greek New Testament."

Scripture scholars also note that writers of the New Testament were brought up to use the Aramaic equivalent of *brothers* to mean both cousins and sons of the same father, as well as other relatives and even nonrelatives. But when the Hebrew Bible was translated into Greek, the translators took an exact equivalent of the Hebrew and failed to make a distinction. The Hebrew word that includes both brothers and cousins was thus translated as *adelphos,* which in Greek usually has the same restricted meaning that the English word *brother* has.

The depiction in the Gospel of John of the Crucifixion also provides important clues as to whether Jesus had brothers in the American sense of the word. Near the cross of Jesus, the Gospel notes, there stood his mother, his mother's sister, Mary the wife of Clopas, and Mary Magdalene. "Seeing his mother there with the disciple whom he loved, Jesus said to his mother, 'Woman, there is your son.' In turn he said to the disciple, 'There is your mother.' From that hour onward, the disciple took her into his care" (John 19:26–27). Setting aside the spiritual dimensions of Jesus' command, and from a strictly practical point of view, as a member of a strong Jewish family, Jesus would have had no right to "give" Mary to one of his disciples if he had had brothers. His brothers would have taken charge of Mary following his death.

Ultimately, as I have stated before, there is no scriptural evidence that can specifically prove or disprove the Catholic position that Mary was perpetually a virgin. As Gilles explains:

> That belief relies not simply on understanding the Hebrew language's lack of a word for "cousin" and the consequent use of the term "brothers" of Jesus, but also on a strong tradition in the early Church that Mary remained a virgin after Jesus' birth. This tradition, like so many others in the early Church, was part of the faith community's earliest belief about Jesus.

In other words, the perpetual virginity of Mary is a matter of faith, a doctrine affirmed in the continuous teaching of the church.

Marian Doctrines: A Hopeful Sign

The church's doctrines on the Virgin Mary are not new Catholic inventions about Mary. They were part of the understanding, the living practice, of the Christian body of believers for centuries before the Protestant Reformation. To cut ourselves off from that early faith community and its understanding of Mary is also to cut ourselves off from the living and developing teachings about Jesus that were set in motion after the death of the apostles. These doctrines on

Mary are based on and directly point to Jesus Christ. They also remind each of us as Christians of the glory that God has promised we will come to know in completeness at the end of time.

Mary does not belong only to Catholics or to any other church or denomination. In recent years, many Protestants have, in fact, embarked on an investigation of historic Christianity that has led them to "rediscover" Mary. In 1999, several theological journals that rarely print articles on Marian devotion published entire issues on the topic. For example, the Marian Library's Mary Page on the Internet notes two such French theological periodicals: *Christus,* whose issue 183 was on "Mary, the One Who Believed"; and *Croire aujourd'hui,* whose issue 61 was devoted to the question of faith and Mary.

There are numerous new books by Protestant pastors and theologians addressing the importance of Mary to the Christian faith. And *Theology Today,* a predominantly Protestant journal from Princeton Theological Seminary, devoted a recent issue to Mary, including an editorial entitled "The Church's First Theologian." "There are many reasons why it is appropriate for a theological journal with a primarily Protestant setting to devote an issue to theological reflection on Mary, the mother of Jesus," observed the editor in the preface to the *Theology Today* editorial. "The significance of Mary for ecumenical discussion, both as a historic source of divisions in the Christian family and, more recently, as a locus of new dialogue among Protestants and Catholics . . . makes her an appropriate topic for a journal devoted to ecumenism." Throughout history, Mary's hymn of praise and thanksgiving—the Magnificat—has been sung in both Catholic and Protestant churches and cathedrals throughout the world as a prayer reflecting piety and faith.

Indeed, there is no greater personal testimony of God's saving power than the reality embodied by Mary of Nazareth, whose entire being "proclaims the greatness of the Lord." Within and through this humble young woman, God's great purpose came to pass, demonstrating that nothing is impossible for God. And as a model of resolute and uncompromising faith worthy of every Christian, this unwed young woman, pregnant with God, continued to proclaim: "my spirit finds joy in God my savior, / For he has looked upon his servant in her lowliness; / all ages to come shall call me blessed. / God who is mighty has done great things for me, / holy is his name" (Luke 1:47–49).

Rather than viewing Mary as a divisive element among Christian faiths, therefore, Pope John Paul II continues to see her as a source of Christian unity—and the Marian feasts celebrated by the church as pointers on our common Christian faith-walk. The proclamation of Mary's Immaculate Conception, for example, points all Christian believers to the fulfillment of God's eternal glory as it will be made manifest in heaven. "As a result, Our Lady, totally preserved from the slavery of evil and the object of God's special favor, anticipates

MARY IN OTHER FAITH TRADITIONS

in her life the path to be taken by the redeemed, the people saved by Christ," the pope remarked in 1998 on the Feast of the Immaculate Conception, December 8.

In much the same manner, remembering Mary's assumption into heaven "is an invitation to look up, to gaze at Mary who is glorified in body, so that we can regain the true meaning of life and be encouraged to walk on its path with trust," said the pope that same year on the Feast of the Assumption. The solemnity of Mary's assumption leads us, points us, to eternity because Mary embodies, through her assumption, our own resurrection. She already has gained what we as Christians all hope and yearn for: to one day be raised up and joined in body and spirit with Christ. In Mary, Catholics and non-Catholics alike can catch a glimpse of the perfect Love we believe we will someday know in heaven. Ultimately, the message of the Feast of the Assumption encourages each of us to consider the value and the deepest meaning of this life on earth, inviting us to transform this world in light of our knowledge of eternity.

What Protestants have had difficulty understanding, explained Lutheran pastor Charles Dickson in his book, *A Protestant Pastor Looks at Mary,* are

> the intentions of Catholic teachings about Mary. In the Immaculate Conception and the Assumption teachings it has not been the intention of the Catholic Church to elevate the Blessed Virgin Mary to deity

status but rather to show her as the shining model of genuinely Christian hope. It is the hope for all humankind. Such a rereading and enlightened understanding on the part of the Protestant community will help to refocus our attention of the entire Christian world on Mary, not as a point of division, but as the real bridge to unity for us all.

Mary can, indeed, be the bridge to unity for Christian believers, if we let her.

When all Christians can see Mary as the radical and foremost model for our pilgrimage of faith, when regardless of our faith tradition we can recognize her as our common mother, when we naturally and without hesitation call on Mary to pray for us and to intercede with her Son on our behalf, then we will allow Mary, the mother of our Savior, to have the prominent place in our faith history that Elizabeth proclaimed she would have: "Blest are you among women and blest is the fruit of your womb. . . . Blest is she who trusted that the Lord's words to her would be fulfilled" (Luke 1:42, 45).

MOTHER! *whose virgin bosom was uncrost*
With the least shade of thought to sin allied;
Woman! above all women glorified,
Our tainted nature's solitary boast;
Purer than foam on central ocean tost;
Brighter than eastern skies at daybreak strewn
With fancied roses, than the unblemished moon
Before her wane begins on heaven's blue coast;
Thy Image falls to earth. Yet some, I ween,
Not unforgiven the suppliant knee might bend,
As to a visible Power, in which did blend
All that was mixed and reconciled in Thee
Of mother's love with maiden purity,
Of high with low, celestial with terrene!

—*WILLIAM WORDSWORTH*
"The Virgin"

CHAPTER FIVE

Mary in Her Apparitions

Now Appearing

As Christians, we often react with embarrassment—and understandably so—at the far-fetched media reports of "miraculous" apparitions: an angel's reflection in someone's soup, a crying image of the Blessed Virgin on a window or on the side of a building. But there are also places such as Lourdes, France, and Fátima, Portugal, where accounts of Mary's apparitions of repentance and hope have not only survived scrutiny, but have also thrived in the life of the church. Nearly eighty thousand visions of Mary have been claimed since the third century a.d., yet less than twenty-two hundred have received official recognition by the Catholic Church.

An apparition is the appearance of a heavenly being— Christ, Mary, a saint, an angel—to a human. A genuine apparition is an outreach by God, and the Bible is full of stories of such instances. God appeared to Adam and Eve in the Garden (Genesis 3). God spoke to Moses through a burning bush (Exodus 3). The prophet Ezekiel saw the chariot of Yahweh (Ezekiel 1). And in the book of Judges, the angel of Yahweh appeared to Gideon (Judges 6). In the New Testament, the angel Gabriel appeared to Mary, announcing the incarnation of Christ (Luke 1:26–28). Angels appeared to the shepherds in the fields, proclaiming the birth of the Messiah (Luke 2:9). And in the Acts of the Apostles, Peter was freed from prison by an angel of the Lord (12:7).

In spite of prevalent skepticism, our American culture seems to retain a dichotomy of opinion regarding spiritual apparitions or interventions. On the one hand, church-accepted apparitions of Mary have been dismissed by many throughout history as hoaxes, and the sites of these apparitions are often regarded as nothing more than dens of commercial opportunity. On the other hand, a glimpse at the current television lineup or a list of recent movies reveals a myriad of TV shows about angels living among us and "true life" reports of everyday miracles, as well as an ample number of Hollywood movies about angels, the afterlife, heaven, ghosts, and heavenly spirits. In fact, reality is full of inexplicable situations. In spite of our elite cultural disbelief and skepticism, there endures a desire for understanding the spiritual reality that surrounds us and that, no matter how hard we try, we cannot entirely rationalize. Yet what our minds cannot comprehend, our hearts often recognize as Truth.

Such can be the case with Marian apparitions.

From the early days of the church, the mother of Jesus was intrinsic in the unfolding story of salvation. From the outset, therefore, it was natural for early Christians not only to use Mary as an example of what it meant to be a follower of Jesus, but also to ask for her intercession before the God who had chosen her. While there have been claims in church history of apparitions of saints or even of Jesus, by far the most frequent reports have involved Mary. Since the Middle Ages, as devotion to the Virgin Mary has grown, so have cases of possible apparitions. This has given the church hierarchy the critical challenge of discerning the authenticity and spiritual nature of apparitions.

According to the University of Dayton's Marian Library Web site, the first testimony of a Marian apparition was recorded by Gregory of Nyssa, who lived in the fourth century. This reported apparition took place in the third century, with Mary appearing to Gregory Thaumaturgus (A.D. 213–70), who was also known as the Miracle Worker. "The vision . . . emphasized Mary's importance in matters of faith. In this vision, Mary, along with John the Evangelist, came to comfort a distressed and confused Gregory on matters of doctrine and spirituality" (Streep, 84).

We do not know much about cases of Marian apparitions in the Middle Ages, although the Marian Library calls the apparitions at the Cistercian monastery of Helfta (thirteenth century) and the visions of St. Bridget of

107

Sweden (1303–73) the two "most interesting cases from the Middles Ages." During the sixteenth century, a new kind of apparition began. Unlike personal apparitions, these apparitions had a public character and "were intended to reanimate faith and to surmount the world's crises," the Mary Page points out. "The most significant case is Guadalupe (1531) which gave birth to a new church on a new continent."

Since World War II, there have been twenty-nine alleged apparitions in the United States alone—from Detroit and Cincinnati to Scottsdale and Sausalito. Most of these apparitions have been rejected as inauthentic or have not yet been recognized.

The Mary Page, maintained on the Internet by the Marian Library, keeps a current list of the numerous reported Marian apparitions of the twentieth century, including date, location, number of people involved, and what decision (if any) has been made by the church concerning its supernatural character. The twentieth century has been rich in reported apparitions of Mary. As the Mary Page notes, "Apparitions of Our Blessed Lady have been reported on every continent on our globe. The seers have been people from many walks of life: men, women, and children. The locations where Marian Apparitions have occurred are numerous: large cities, remote areas, caves, churches, fields, homes, monasteries, and other places." The Mary Page statistics also indicate that in the twentieth century alone there have been 386 cases of Marian apparitions. Of the supernatural character of 299 of these cases, the church has as yet made no decision, either because the local bishop is studying the case or because the church has not yet begun to study it. In only eight of these 386 cases has the church officially decided that there is a supernatural character to the apparitions, the local bishops then granting approval of faith expression (prayer and devotion) in connection with them. These eight cases are Fátima, Portugal; Beauraing, Belgium; Banneaux, Belgium; Akita, Japan; Syracuse, Italy; Zeitoun, Egypt; Manila, Philippines (according to some sources); and Betania, Venezuela. Yet reports of Mary's visitations continue.

To Believe or Not to Believe

It is important to note that belief in the apparitions of Mary is not regarded by the church as a matter of faith or morals. This means that belief in Marian apparitions is only permitted, not required. In matters of faith, the Catholic Church distinguishes between two kinds of revelations. First, there are the revelations that have come to us from Christ— and through the prophets before him and the apostles after him—which make up an unchanged body of teachings called the "deposit of the faith." These are called "public" revelations because Christ said they were to be given to all peoples. "This good news of the kingdom will be proclaimed throughout the world as a witness to all the nations" (Matthew 24:14).

With the death of the last apostle, public revelations ended. Everything that God needed to reveal had already been revealed through Christ. Nothing needed to be added. The church teaches that "no new public revelation is to be expected before the glorious manifestations of our Lord Jesus Christ. Yet even if Revelation is already complete, it has not been made completely explicit; it remains for Christian faith gradually to grasp its full significance over the course of the centuries" (Catechism, 66). Apparitions are, by contrast, considered "private" revelations. Private revelations are always a reminder given to an individual person of some part of public revelation given by God—sometimes by way of an angel, or a saint, or Mary, his own mother. A genuine apparition will never be anything other than a private revelation, and it will never convey a new or revised public revelation. "It is not their role to improve or complete Christ's definitive Revelation, but to help us live more fully by it in a certain period of history" (Catechism, 67).

Belief in Marian apparitions is only permitted, not required.

No apparition, therefore, is necessary to complete the substance of the faith. When the church defines an apparition as "worthy of belief," a person is free to believe it or not. It is the believer's decision to accept or reject the reminder that its message conveys, which is always meant to

MARY IN HER APPARITIONS

bring attention back to faith in Christ. The message of a genuine apparition cannot in any way be contrary to the teachings of the church.

Why Do We Need Apparitions?

While the faith has been revealed in its completeness, our understanding and awareness of this truth is forever blooming. God reaches out to each of us every day, yet how we interpret or recognize these messages is a matter of personal conviction and awareness. As a body of believers, Christians have always had a strong need to experience Mary in the midst of daily life and, in a special way, in times of affliction and need. It is not surprising, then, that visitations by Mary, our mediator and intercessor, are frequently connected with some kind of crisis. The apparitions at Fátima, for example, took place during the First World War. In 1933, the year that Adolf Hitler was appointed chancellor of Germany and the global economy underwent disarray, there were Marian apparitions at Banneaux and Beauraing in Belgium. Mary was also reportedly seen in fifteen other apparitions throughout the European continent.

Most genuine apparitions of Mary—those officially recognized and validated by the church—bring some special message to the world through the words of the Blessed Mother. Throughout history, the messages that Mary has spoken to believers have been substantially the same: calls for a return to prayer and for penance, sacrifice, and personal conversion.

As with Jesus' befriending of tax collectors and sinners, apparitions don't come only to exceptional people. Bernadette, for example, was a remarkably sweet-natured child before Mary appeared to her at Lourdes. But at the time when Mary chose her, Bernadette was totally ignorant of her catechism and not unusually pious. As with God's messages to reluctant prophets in the Old Testament, apparitions often come to people who don't want them before they happen, who later wish they hadn't had them, or who don't want to acknowledge them at all. Yet the modesty of these people's conduct should be a testimony in itself, set in contrast to false or fraudulent self-proclaimed visionaries who may routinely bless people, claim to cure pilgrims, or desire to be interviewed about their alleged visions.

Studied apparitions are classified as one of the following: "not worthy of belief," "not contrary to the faith," or "worthy of belief." Silence from the local bishop is really an indication that an alleged apparition deserves no notice. In fact, the most that any apparition officially gets from the church is a negative approval, an official declaration that there is nothing in the report or in its implications that is contrary to the faith, misguided, or harmful to the faithful, and this makes it "worthy of belief." A classification of "not worthy of belief" indicates that the local bishop has identified

MARY IN HER APPARITIONS

some problem with the apparition, leading him to conclude that it does not have a supernatural character.

Because of the obvious effects that the announcement of a genuine apparition has on the life of the church, both local and universal, the church thoroughly investigates every report to determine its authenticity. The investigation process begins with the local bishop, who appoints a committee to take testimony, investigate, study, and report its findings to the bishop. Reports that have enough substance to merit official examination are studied by panels of qualified experts—theologians, scientists, medical doctors—who are assembled by the local bishop, the only person authorized by law to investigate. If the bishop concludes that the apparition's character is supernatural, it means that the case cannot be explained away as a result of an impediment in the visionary, as fraud, as a natural phenomenon, or as an occurrence of demonic origin. Of the many apparent apparitions, few have been eventually deemed worthy of belief by the church, and then only after much waiting and careful investigation into the events and the results of its devotion.

God reaches out to each of us every day, yet how we interpret or recognize these messages is a matter of personal conviction and awareness.

Medjugorje: A Good Example

The alleged apparitions of the Blessed Virgin Mary to six young people at Medjugorje, Bosnia-Herzegovina, have been a source of interest and controversy since they were first reported in June of 1981. The apparitions, which the children said first began in a hillside field near the village, moved to the church of St. James in Medjugorje, located in the Catholic Croatian region of what was formerly Yugoslavia.

Reports say that the young visionaries saw, heard, and even touched Mary during their visions. The reports maintain that Mary relayed ten secret messages related to coming world events and that each child received several or all ten of them. According to the visionaries, Mary called for greater faith, urging peace through prayer, fasting, penance, and personal conversion.

The first vision occurred on June 24, 1981, when four young people, two of them from Medjugorje and two of them from Sarajevo, were walking along the lower slopes of the Crnica Mountains. These three girls and one boy saw a bright light shining from the mountainside. Within the light, they saw the figure of a young woman holding a child. Although the figure called out to them, the children ran away in fear. The next day, the children returned, bringing two more children with them. Again they saw a blue-eyed, dark-haired woman with twelve gold stars encircling her head and an infant in her arms. On the third day, the children returned with nearly all the villagers. At 6:40 P.M., they saw the lady, this time standing on a cloud before them. One of the children challenged the apparition with holy water, demanding that it disappear if it was from Satan. Instead, the children heard the lady urge them not to be afraid, saying, "I am the Virgin Mary." She told them that she had come in peace to call for conversion and reconciliation. Since then, the seers have reported seeing Mary regularly and, eventually, infrequently; singly and together; at church, on the hillside, and in their homes. Like other seers, they say they have received secrets from Mary, some personal and some apocalyptic in nature. Millions of pilgrims continue to visit this war-torn region, noting numerous instances of visual phenomena as well as stories of personal conversion and healing.

An investigative commission appointed by former local bishop Pavao Zanic of Mostar-Duvno reported in March 1984 that the authenticity of the apparitions had not been established and that cases of reported healing had not been verified. He dismissed the apparitions as a case of "collective hallucination." Former archbishop Frane Franic of Split-Makarska, on the other hand, said in December 1985 that "speaking as a believer and not as a bishop," his personal conviction was that the events at Medjugorje were "of supernatural inspiration."

As is the case in any reported Marian apparition, the church is currently studying the events reported at Medjugorje before making a declaration regarding their authenticity, and no official announcement is expected soon. The church's exploration into whether supernatural apparitions are involved at Medjugorje involves not only the apparitions themselves, but also external ramifications, such as the spiritual development of the six young people, the increases in Mass attendance, sacramental practice at the scene of the apparitions, and the incidence of reconciliation and devotion among visitors and locals. In 1986, John Paul II approved travel to Medjugorje for prayer, fasting, and conversion. By the early 1990s, pilgrimages were disrupted by the violent civil war taking place in the region.

Historically, the time it takes to grant full recognition to apparitions by the Virgin Mary varies but always takes place after the conclusion of the official process of studying the apparition. Fátima was formally recognized thirteen years after the events, while Guadalupe's acceptance was delayed two hundred years.

One reliable test of any apparition is whether or not the reported message of Mary is in agreement with the Bible and is consistent with the teaching of the church. Since "by their fruits you will know them," the fruits of an apparition on the devotion of the community and on the pilgrims to the site are also relevant. Some of the positive signs might include repentance, revival, healings, renewed faith, return to the church, Bible reading, and manifestation of various gifts of the Spirit.

Claims of apparitions of the Blessed Virgin Mary and investigations of alleged apparitions are currently taking place in Ireland, Italy, Belgium, Canada, and the United States. Whatever one's personal belief may be, the history of the apparitions of the Blessed Virgin Mary undoubtedly provides matter for reflection on popular religion, divine intervention, personal experience, and the meaning of revelation. Of the number of Marian apparitions that have been officially recognized as "worthy of belief" by the church, five of the more popular and well-known apparitions are discussed here.

Our Lady of Guadalupe, Mexico

On December 9, 1531, an Aztec Indian convert whose Christian name was Juan Diego and whose indigenous name was Singing Eagle set out before dawn to walk fifteen miles to Tlaltelolco, Mexico, to attend Mass. As he was passing the foot of Tepeyac Hill, consecrated to the Mother Goddess of the Aztecs, he saw at the summit a brilliant light and a glowing cloud encircled by a rainbow, and then he heard celestial music. Filled with wonder, Juan Diego stood still in silence. Then he heard a woman's voice speaking in his Indian language, asking him to ascend the hill. When Juan Diego reached the top, he saw a beautiful young lady standing in the midst of a glorious light and dressed like an Aztec princess.

The lady told Juan Diego, in his native language, that she was the "Holy Mary, the eternal Virgin, Mother of the true." She told him of her desire to have a shrine built there where she could manifest her love, compassion, comfort, and protection. "I am your merciful Mother," she said, "thine, and all the dwellers of this earth. To bring to pass what I bid thee, go thou and speak to the Bishop of Mexico and say I sent thee to make manifest to him my will."

The bishop was kind but skeptical and sent Juan Diego back to get proof of the lady's identity. The lady agreed to give the proof on the following morning, but Juan Diego's uncle fell seriously ill. Juan Diego, thinking it more important to go get a priest for his uncle, tried taking a different route to the church in order to avoid meeting the lady, but she met him on the path and told him that his uncle had been cured. She then told Juan Diego to climb to the top of the hill where they had first met. There, Juan Diego was surprised to find roses growing in the frosty December ground, and he collected them in his *tilma* (or mantle) to take to the bishop. When Juan Diego opened his *tilma* to give the bishop the flowers he had collected on the hill, a glowing life-size figure of the Virgin miraculously appeared on the *tilma*. The bishop was immediately convinced of the genuineness of the apparition by the evidence of the figure, an image that is revered to this day as the imprint of Our Lady of Guadalupe. Soon after that, a church was built on the site where the lady and Juan Diego had met, and thousands of Aztec Indians converted to Christianity.

Mary appeared a total of four times in 1531 to Juan Diego (declared Blessed in 1990) on Tepeyac Hill, about five miles north of Mexico City. The bishop, who did not know the Indian's language, heard Juan Diego name the lady Santa María Coatlaxopeuh, which sounded to him like Santa María de Guadalupe, the name of a famous shrine in Spain, and this then became her name. Juan Diego's mantle, which has remained bright and clear for more than four centuries, has been preserved and is enshrined above the altar in the Basilica of Our Lady of Guadalupe in Mexico City. This mantle is handwoven from the fibers of the maguey cactus, which have an ordinary life span of twenty years. The portrait on the mantle of our Lady is that of a four-foot-eight-inch-tall, brown-skinned maiden wearing a pink robe and a turquoise mantle covered with stars and outlined in gold. The lady in the image is surrounded by rays of light and is supported by a crescent moon, beneath which is the figure of a small person.

In a 1754 decree, Pope Benedict XIV named Mary the patroness of New Spain and authorized a Mass and Office under the title of Our Lady of Guadalupe for celebration on December 12. Our Lady of Guadalupe was designated patroness of Latin America by St. Pius X in 1910 and of all the Americas by Pius XII in 1945.

It is impossible to measure in concrete terms the full impact of Our Lady of Guadalupe on Mexico and Latin America. For Mexicans, Nuestra Señora de Guadalupe is much more than their country's patroness; *la virgencita* is truly a national symbol claimed by all Mexicans, whether Catholic or evangelical. It is true that the appearance of the olive-skinned lady who spoke the Indians' native language initiated many rapid conversions of the native Aztecs to Catholicism. But perhaps the most remarkable and revolutionary aspect of the first apparition of Mary in the New World is that the Aztec Indian identity of Juan Diego's Mary validated and empowered the native inhabitants' sense of culture and heritage. This is an image of Mary's aligning herself with the lowly, the simple of the earth, again bringing to life the words she once proclaimed to Elizabeth in a canticle:

> My being proclaims the greatness of the Lord,
>> my spirit finds joy in God my savior.
> For he has looked upon his servant in her lowliness. . . .
> He has shown mighty with his arm;
>> he has confused the proud in their inmost thoughts.
> He has deposed the mighty from their thrones
>> and raised the lowly to high places.
> (Luke 1:46–48, 51–52)

This empathy, this identification with and understanding of the situation, feelings, and motives of those who are seen as the least in this world is the greatest gift of Our Lady of Guadalupe. It has, no doubt, transformed and challenged the hearts of many.

Our Lady of Lourdes, France

Perhaps the most famous of the apparitions of the Virgin Mary are those to fourteen-year-old Bernadette Soubirous, a girl who spoke the native Bigourdian dialect of her region and who could neither read nor write. Bernadette's hometown of Lourdes is situated at the foot of the Pyrenees in southwest France and had approximately four thousand inhabitants when she lived there. Bernadette was born on January 7, 1844, to François and Louise Soubirous. Although her family experienced few hardships in the first twelve years of her life, they later fell into dire poverty. With nowhere else to turn, the family moved into an old prison, abandoned and closed because of its poor condition.

On February 11, 1858, Bernadette joined her sister Toinette and their friend Jeanne on a trip to the foothills in search of firewood for the family. When they arrived at a nearby river, Toinette and Jeanne began taking off their shoes to cross the water. Bernadette, because she suffered from asthma, decided not to risk her health by exposing her feet to the icy water. As she looked around for a shallow place to cross, Bernadette suddenly heard a rustling sound of wind behind her. She turned around to see a beautiful white-clad

121

young woman wearing an azure sash and yellow shoes. The smiling woman was standing in front of a grotto and was enveloped by a golden cloud.

The lady beckoned for Bernadette to approach and signaled with the rosary that hung on her arm for Bernadette to begin to pray. After Bernadette had said the rosary, the lady and the cloud disappeared into the grotto. Three days later, Bernadette returned to the grotto of Massabielle with several young girls after Sunday Mass, each girl carrying a bottle of holy water from church. As the girls began to say the rosary, the woman appeared to Bernadette, still saying nothing. On February 18, Bernadette returned to the site, accompanied this time by two adults. As they recited the rosary, the woman—whom Bernadette simply called *aquero,* or "that one," in her native dialect—appeared to Bernadette and asked, "Would you do me the kindness of coming here for fifteen days?"

Each morning at six o'clock Bernadette visited the grotto, kneeling in prayer. Each time, those who were present were moved by Bernadette's appearance during the visions, noting that she took on a beautiful radiance. Our Lady's messages to Bernadette were simple, such as, "I do not promise to make you happy in this world but in the other" and "Penance, penance, penance, pray for sinners." On February 25, the lady told Bernadette to "go to the spring, drink of it, and wash yourself there," directing her to a specific spot on the ground where Bernadette immediately began scraping away at the wet dirt. A spring miraculously came forth from the site where our Lady had told Bernadette to dig. During the thirteenth apparition, our Lady said to Bernadette, "Go, tell the priests to come here in procession and build a chapel here."

Our Lady repeatedly invited Bernadette to pray, recommending penance and prayer for all people as the only way to obtain pardon for the sins of humankind. She identified herself in Bernadette's local dialect by saying, "I am the Immaculate Conception," words that the uneducated young Bernadette could not understand, but that were very meaningful to the local priest. The story of Lourdes increased the commitment of the faithful to belief in the Immaculate Conception of Mary, which had been proclaimed as an official teaching of the church just four years before the apparitions began.

Mary appeared to Bernadette eighteen times at the grotto of Massabielle, near Lourdes, between February 11 and July 16, 1858. Mary's request that a chapel be built at the grotto and spring was fulfilled in 1862, and devotion under the title of Our Lady of Lourdes was authorized, with a February 11 feast instituted by Leo XIII to commemorate the apparitions. Bernadette Soubirous later became a nun, joining the Sisters of Charity in Nevers, France, in 1866, and taking the religious name Marie-Bernard. She was ill for the rest of her life, and she died in 1879 on April 16, which is now her feast day. Bernadette was canonized a saint in 1933 on the Feast of the Immaculate Conception, December 8. Her incorrupt body still rests in a glass reliquary at the chapel of St. Gildard in Nevers.

Since March 1, 1858, the church has recognized sixty-five miracles from the waters at Lourdes, and there have been another five thousand "inexplicable healings." Approximately five million pilgrims from 150 countries visit this town of 15,300 inhabitants every year, making Lourdes one of the most important cities in France in the hotel trade, second only to Paris.

Our Lady of Banneaux and Our Lady of Beauraing, Belgium

On May 21, 1983, Pope John Paul II visited the shrine of Our Lady of Banneaux, near Liège, Belgium, and declared, "The Virgin of the Poor has invited us to come here; being conscious that her motherly regard rests on us, we will spiritually renew ourselves by discovering again the deep sense of the messianic message, implied in the eight Beatitudes of Christ."

Between January 15 and March 2, 1933, Mary appeared eight times to an eleven-year-old peasant girl named Mariette Beco in the garden behind her family cottage in Banneaux. On a cold January night, Mariette stood near the kitchen window, watching and waiting for her younger brother Julien to return home. Instead, Mariette, the oldest of four children living in this small, poor home, saw a glowing figure standing motionless near the family's vegetable garden, a few yards away from the house. The figure was that of a lady dressed in a flowing white gown and veil and a brilliant blue sash, holding a rosary in her right hand and nodding and smiling at Mariette. When Mariette told her mother about the lady outside, her mother locked the door and forbade her to go out, fearful that the woman was a witch or a ghost.

Three nights later, Mariette went outside, knelt on the frozen ground, and prayed the rosary, hoping that the lady would return. When she opened her arms in a gesture of welcome, the lady appeared, gradually coming closer until she was only a few feet from the child. After Mariette prayed silently for twenty minutes, the lady motioned for her to come to a nearby spot, where Mariette began digging with her hands and discovered an unknown spring. The lady then spoke for the first time, asking Mariette to plunge her hands into the water and saying, "This spring is reserved for me," a remark she affirmed in other apparitions. During the next few apparitions, the lady said that the spring was "reserved for all nations, to cure the sick," and she told Mariette, "I come to alleviate suffering," "Believe in me, I will believe in you." Finally, she requested simply, "Pray earnestly."

The lady called herself the Virgin of the Poor and has since been venerated as Our Lady of the Poor, the Sick, and the Indifferent. A small chapel was blessed on August 15, 1933. Numerous miracles have been recorded at Banneaux's spring, where thousands of pilgrims visit every year to be healed physically and spiritually. Approval of devotion to Our Lady of Banneaux was granted in 1949 by Bishop Louis J. Kerkhofs of Liège. A statue of that title was solemnly crowned in 1956.

Within days of the visions at Banneaux, Mary appeared thirty-three times between November 29, 1932, and January 3, 1933, in Beauraing, a small town in the French-speaking part of Belgium. Once again, Mary appeared to children, this time to five children ranging in age from nine to fifteen.

Outside a school run by the Sisters of Christian Doctrine in Beauraing, Fernande and Albert Voisin stood waiting for their sister Gilberte along with two friends, Andree Degeimbre and his sister, also named Gilberte. When they saw a bright light moving by the viaduct above the street, all the children looked up at the viaduct, where, instead of the reflection of car headlights, they saw a lady dressed in a white dress, whom they immediately recognized as the Virgin Mary. The children were so agitated that they pounded on the door of the school, but the sister who opened the door could see nothing on the bridge where the children were pointing. When Gilberte Voisin came out, she too saw the lady. Their parents dismissed the story, thinking the children were playing a prank.

The next day, as the four again waited for Gilberte after school, they saw the figure of the lady in white. They ran to the Degeimbre house, where Mme Degeimbre decided that someone was playing tricks on the children. She decided to accompany the children the next day—with a stick, to punish whoever was responsible. The children once again saw the lady, this time crowned with golden rays, but Mme Degeimbre saw nothing. For several days, every time the children appeared at the site, so did the lady. The parents became convinced of the veracity of the apparitions, not by anything they saw but by the evidence of the children's transformation.

The number of spectators grew as doctors, police, and psychologists, all wishing to test the truthfulness of the children's account, came to see them. During the apparitions, the lady asked that a chapel be built and identified herself as "the Immaculate Conception." She exhorted the children to pray, and when asked what she wanted, the lady replied, "That you always be good." During the final apparition on January 3, 1933, each of the five children received a separate message, and three of them were entrusted with a secret. The lady also exposed her radiant heart, shining with light and love.

While the seers remained practicing Catholics, all of them married and lived secular lives. Reserved approval of devotion to Our Lady of Beauraing was given on February 2, 1943, while Belgium was under German occupation. Final authorization was granted on July 2, 1949, by Bishop Charue of Namur. A chapel was erected and consecrated in the garden of the convent school in 1954.

Our Lady of Fátima, Portugal

In May of 1917, the third year of the First World War, Portugal was fighting alongside France, Great Britain, and the United States against the Germans. Pope Benedict XV wrote a pastoral letter urging the children of the world to appeal to Mary, mother of mercy, for peace. On the thirteenth day of that same month, our Lady appeared to three young Portuguese shepherd children, Lucia dos Santos (ten years old) and her cousins Francisco Marto (nine) and his sister Jacinta (seven).

One clear Sunday morning, the three children were tending their sheep in the valley of Cova da Iria, near Fátima, when they saw a sudden flash of lightning, followed by a great ball of light that came toward them and transformed into a beautiful woman wearing a brilliant white dress. The lady, a rosary on her right hand, was smiling, and she told the children not to be afraid. Lucia asked the lady where she came from, to which the lady replied, "I come from heaven." When asked if they would go to heaven, the lady replied, "Yes," but said that Francisco would have to say many rosaries.

The lady instructed the children to come back to that same place on the thirteenth day of every month until October. She also asked them to pray the rosary every day and to accept all the suffering that God might send. A month later the children returned, this time accompanied by some sixty people. Lucia began to recite the rosary, and the lady again appeared, confiding in her that Francisco and Jacinta would soon go to heaven, but that Lucia would remain on earth to promote devotion to the lady's immaculate heart. The witnesses could not see the apparition but reported seeing a tree's branches bent as if weighted down. All heard a loud sound, like that of a rocket taking off, which marked the end of the vision.

Many officials and observers were skeptical about the children's claims, so during the July 13 visit Lucia begged the lady for a miracle that all could see. The Virgin promised she would perform one, along with disclosing her identity, at their October visit. The three children were taken into custody by local authorities on August 13 and thrown into jail, but they refused to recant their visions. Three days later, the children returned home, unharmed. On August 17, Mary appeared again.

Mary's messages to the children were mainly requests for the frequent recitation of the rosary. She also encouraged the practice of mortification for the conversion of sinners, called for devotion to herself under the title of her Immaculate Heart, asked that the people of Russia be consecrated to her under this title, and asked that the faithful make a communion of reparation on the first Saturday of each month.

On October 13, 1917, the lady identified herself to the children as Our Lady of the Rosary, asking that a chapel be constructed at that site. She also called the people of the world to repentance for their sins and asked that people say the rosary every day. The crowd of approximately seventy thousand people saw and heard nothing. Then our Lady performed the miracle of the sun. The sun lost its color, became a silver disk in a multicolored sky, and began to dance in the sky as the crowd screamed in terror, wept, and prayed. The sun zigzagged through the sky for ten minutes, stopping three times before assuming its place in the sky again. While the crowd contemplated the sun, the three children received four consecutive visions: the sacred family, Jesus joyfully giving his blessing to the world, Our Lady of Sorrows, and Our Lady of Mount Carmel with a scapular in her hand.

Mary had appeared to the children six times between May 13 and October 13, 1917. As predicted, both Francisco and Jacinta died within a few years of the apparitions. Francisco died in 1919, and his sister Jacinta died in 1920, both of influenza. Lucia joined the Sisters of St. Dorothy in 1926 and became a Carmelite nun in 1948. She is still alive, living in a cloistered Carmelite convent in Portugal.

The apparitions at Fátima were declared authentic by the bishop of Leiria and declared worthy of belief on October 13, 1930. Devotion to Our Lady of Fátima was authorized under the title of Our Lady of the Rosary, with a feast day of October 7. In October 1942, Pius XII consecrated the world to Mary under the title of her Immaculate Heart. Ten years later, in the first apostolic letter addressed directly to the peoples of Russia, he consecrated them in a special manner to Mary.

During the apparitions at Fátima, the children received three secrets, which the Virgin entrusted to Lucia dos Santos, the principal and longest-living seer. In 1927, Lucia revealed the first two secrets in a memoir. First, she described the vision of hell that the three children had been shown in 1917, noting that only devotion to Mary's Immaculate Heart could save sinners. She also said that a second, more terrible world war would take place. The second secret warned that if Russia was not converted, it would spread its errors throughout the world, and many different nations would be annihilated.

The third secret, however, Lucia wrote down and did not disclose. She asked that it not be revealed before 1960. The handwritten text of this third secret of Fátima, which had been kept at the Vatican since 1957, was finally published by the Vatican in June of the Jubilee Year 2000. The forty-three-page booklet includes Pope John Paul II's interpretation of the secret: that it is a symbolic prophecy of the church's twentieth-century struggles with evil political systems and of its ultimate triumph. The pope, who credits Our Lady of Fátima with saving his life when he was shot in St. Peter's Square in Rome, also believes the vision referred specifically to this 1981 attempt on his life.

The Vatican's booklet on the third secret of Fátima describes Lucia's final vision of "a bishop dressed in white, we had the impression it was the Holy Father," going up a steep mountain toward "a big cross of rough-hewn trunks" with other bishops, priests, and religious. "Before reaching there, the Holy Father passed through a big city half in ruins and prayed for the souls of the corpses he met on his way," Lucia wrote. "Having reached the top of the mountain, on his knees at the foot of the big cross he was killed by a group of soldiers who fired bullets and arrows at him." The others walking with the pope were also killed, and angels standing beneath the cross gathered the blood of the martyrs, put it in "a crystal aspersorium" as if it were holy water, "and with it sprinkled the souls that were making their way to God."

As with any other private revelation approved by the church, the Fátima secret, with its message and interpretation, is meant to help Catholics in living their faith, but Catholics are not obliged to believe or use it. In October 1999, the pope approved the last document needed for the beatification of Francisco and Jacinta Marto, and they were beatified on May 13, 2000. They are the youngest people to be beatified since the modern canonization process began in 1592.

Why do you stand looking up at the sky?—Acts 1:11

It wasn't just wind chasing
thin, gunmetal clouds
across a loud sky;
and it wasn't the feeling that one might ascend
on that excited air,
rising like a trumpet note,
and it wasn't just my sister's water breaking,
her crying out,
the downward draw of blood and bone . . .
It was all of that,
mud and new grass
pushing up through melting snow,
the lilac in bud by my front door
bent low
by last week's ice storm.
Now the new mother, that leaky vessel,
begins to nurse her child,
beginning the long good-bye.

—*KATHLEEN NORRIS*
"Ascension" (from *Little Girls in Church*)

CHAPTER SIX

Mary in Prayer—Popular Devotion

Marian Devotion

As early as the third century, Christian believers requested the intercession of Mary, the mother of God, by using a popular prayer of petition. Known in Latin as *Sub Tuum Praesidium*, the prayer was first found on a Greek papyrus in the third century and is the oldest known prayer to Mary.

> We turn to you for protection,
> holy Mother of God.
> Listen to our prayers
> and help us in our needs.
> Save us from every danger,
> glorious and blessed Virgin.

Marian devotions have a strong scriptural basis and a long history in the church. Since early Christians saw a natural connection between Mary and her Son, honoring

Jesus' mother was a prominent way to preserve what they knew and proclaimed as truth about her Son: he was conceived of the Holy Spirit, and from the moment of his conception he was fully human and fully divine. From the beginning, therefore, Marian devotion and Marian prayers pointed to Jesus and to the truths necessary for our salvation. In them, Mary was proclaimed a faithful disciple and was held up as the perfect example for all believers.

These same precepts were reiterated by the Second Vatican Council in the document *Lumen Gentium*: "Mary was involved in the mystery of Christ. As the most holy Mother of God she was, after her Son, exalted by divine grace above all angels and men." This is why the church appropriately honors Mary with special reverence and has, from ancient times, venerated her under the title of "God bearer." The church has endorsed many forms of piety toward the mother of God, always provided "that they were within the limits of sound and orthodox doctrine." Let the faithful remember, the church emphasized in the Vatican II document, "that true devotion consists neither in fruitless and passing emotion, nor in a certain vain credulity. Rather, it proceeds from the true faith." It is through this faith that we are led to know the mother of God. And it is in faith that we are moved to a relationship with her as our mother and to the imitation of her virtues.

The Liturgy of the Hours, or Divine Office, is the public prayer of the church for praising God and sanctifying the day,

MARY IN PRAYER—POPULAR DEVOTION

and it is the paradigm of Marian prayer and devotion. To "say," or celebrate, the Divine Office daily is a sacred obligation for men in holy orders and for men and women religious who have professed solemn vows. Using a book called the breviary, they meditate on the psalms and on readings from Scripture. As the sun sets, the Marian aspects of the Divine Office become more pronounced. Every evening, in convents, monasteries, and homes around the world, the faithful recite Mary's canticle (Luke 1:46–55), remembering with Mary that our souls are called to proclaim God's goodness and rejoicing with her because God has looked on us with favor. As dusk leads to night, we end our night prayer and proceed to our beds reciting any one of a number of antiphons to honor Mary.

Although in modern times the celebration of the Divine Office is highly commended and encouraged for all the community of the faithful, it was, at one point in history, inaccessible to the laity, most of whom could not read or write. With time constraints and illiteracy keeping many of the faithful from participating in this aspect of the church's life, the people turned to simpler forms of devotion. Some of these, such as the Angelus and the rosary, developed historically as a sort of layperson's breviary. Since the laypeople could not read the psalms, they needed a prayer that could be easily remembered. Eventually, the Hail Marytook the place of the written prayer texts used by the more educated clergy. Much like the Divine Office for professed religious men and women, these devotions

137

promoted daily meditation on important events in Jesus' life as well as prayer at specific moments throughout the day.

The Hail Mary

> Hail Mary,
> full of grace,
> the Lord is with you.
> Blessed are you among women,
> and blessed is the fruit of your womb, Jesus.
> Holy Mary, Mother of God,
> pray for us sinners
> now and at the hour of our death.

The Hail Mary, also known as the Ave Maria ("Hail Mary" in Latin) or as the "angelic salutation," breaks down into three parts. The first part of the Hail Mary, straight out of St. Luke's infancy narrative, appeared in liturgies as early as the sixth century. They are the words of the archangel Gabriel to Mary at the Annunciation: "Hail Mary, full of grace, the Lord is with you. Blessed are you among women." Our prayer echoes across time and history, merging with the greeting of the angel to the one who was found full of grace because the Lord was with her and within her. Along with the angel, we too call her blessed among all women because she believed in God's saving power and chose to say yes to grace being born in her.

The second part, the words said by Mary's cousin Elizabeth on Mary's visitation (Luke 1:42), were added to the first part by about the year 1000: "and blessed is the fruit of your womb, [Jesus]."

The only additions to these two verses are the names of Jesus and Mary, which simply make it clear to whom one is referring. We turn to Mary because, as the mother of God, as the mother of our Savior and brother, she is our mother too. As I say the words of the Hail Mary daily, calling her full of grace and proclaiming that the Lord is with her, I remember that I too, as a Christian, am called to let Jesus, the source of all grace, be born in me. In this way, Mary continues to be my ultimate example. In her, the first Christian, we see ourselves as we desire to be and we ask for her intercession. This idea makes up the third part of the prayer: "Holy Mary, Mother of God, pray for us sinners now and at the hour of our death."

While this last part of the Hail Mary is not from Scripture, its thoughts are entirely biblical. Not only as the first Christian, but also as the mother of Jesus the Christ, Mary is certainly worthy of being called holy. And as I have discussed already, reference to Mary as the mother of God—a truth proclaimed by Christians in the early centuries—points to the divine One who was born of her. She was, indeed, the mother of our God, who became man in Jesus.

Finally, we ask Mary to pray for us before her Son, to intercede on our behalf, in much the same way that we ask those who are close to us to say a prayer of petition or thanksgiving on our behalf. Who can better pray for us than the mother of our Savior?

> Because she gives us Jesus, her son, Mary is Mother of God and our mother; we can entrust all our cares and petitions to her: she prays for us as she prayed for herself: "Let it be done to me according to your word." By entrusting ourselves to her prayer, we abandon ourselves to the will of God together with her: "Thy will be done." (Catechism, 2677)

We know that this request for intercession also applies to the saints in heaven, who, as Revelation 5:8 notes, intercede for us by offering our prayers to God: "The twenty-four elders fell down before the Lamb . . . holding vessels of gold filled with aromatic spices, which were the prayers of God's holy people."

The first two salutations of the Hail Mary were joined in the formulas of the Eastern Rite by the sixth century and were similarly used in Rome in the seventh century. Church historians believe that the first half of the Hail Mary was prayed commonly and began to take on the spiritual significance of other common prayers, such as the Our Father and the Apostles' Creed, toward the end of the twelfth century. Pope Urban IV probably inserted the name of Jesus at the conclusion of the salutations around 1262. The present form of the petition was incorporated into the Liturgy of the Hours in 1514, and it was officially incorporated into the reformed breviary of Pope Pius V in 1568.

In 1825, the Austrian classical composer Franz Schubert, a Catholic, set to music a portion of Sir Walter Scott's verses from "The Lady of the Lake." Sometime later, it was noted that the Latin text of the Hail Mary could be sung to the music, and the two were brought together. Some believe it was the Hail Mary that originally inspired Schubert to compose the beautiful creation known simply as the "Ave Maria." Of the many musical settings of this ancient prayer, the "Ave Maria" of Franz Schubert is perhaps the most widely known.

The Rosary

A few years ago, woven bracelets with the initials "WWJD"—for "What would Jesus do?"—became the rage for Christian teenagers. It wasn't long before the bracelets were followed by all sorts of WWJD paraphernalia—earrings, necklaces, T-shirts, bookmarks, posters, rings—easily found at both Christian and secular stores. In a very real way, these four letters became not only an emblem for Christians announcing a personal desire to follow the way of Christ, but also a prayer that the wearer's actions and words might indeed follow in Jesus' footsteps. While the WWJD bracelets are a contemporary fad, the craze is rooted in an instinctive desire of humans to intertwine faith and life, a need the rosary has answered for centuries.

In popular culture, perhaps no item is more emblematic of Catholics and the Catholic faith than the rosary. Even non-Catholics are familiar with the beaded "necklace," usually associating it with the image of a decorative object hanging from a rearview mirror, or a grandmother silently moving her lips while fingering the beads. In the last few years, the rosary as a form of prayer has become popular not only with Catholics—who are rediscovering it—but also with many Protestants, who recognize it as a Scripture-based prayer exercise. A few years ago, my roommate at a Christian writers' retreat was a Protestant mother named Neel who loved Mary. Neel shared with me that she had taught herself how to pray the rosary because of its spiritual richness. The rosary not only reminded her of specific moments in Jesus' life, but also allowed her to meditate on their significance. In a very intimate way, Neel reminded me of the rosary's profound and personal spiritual substance.

My first memories of saying the rosary are tied to my grandmother Josefa, who never went to bed at night without reciting the rosary. On special occasions or when she felt a need for more communal intercession on behalf of a family member or friend, Josefita, as she was lovingly called by those who knew her, would gather our family into the living room to pray the rosary. Most nights, I would simply hear from Josefita's room the quiet whispers of my grandmother saying the rosary. To this day, whether I hear or say the rosary in Spanish or English, I can still hear her quiet voice in my ear, no doubt joining me in prayer from heaven even now. Such is the power and transcendence of the communion of saints.

The rosary, considered a private or extraliturgical prayer of the church, is one of the most ancient prayer forms. The religious exercise of reciting prayers while following a string of beads or a knotted cord is, in fact, widespread among the major religious groups, occurring not only in the Christian tradition but also in Hinduism, Buddhism, and Islam. In the Christian church, the practice began in the early days of Christianity, apparently originating among early monks and hermits, who used a piece of heavy cord knotted at intervals as an aid to recite their shorter prayers.

Also called the Psalter of Mary, the rosary parallels the form of the Psalter (the 150 psalms of the Bible). As the online Catholic Encyclopedia notes, the rosary is "the prayer of the people adapted alike for the use of simple and learned." It was the laity's desire to share in the church's daily prayer, the Liturgy of the Hours, that prompted the development of the rosary. Like the Liturgy of the Hours and its movement through the 150 psalms, the rosary began as a movement through 150 Our Fathers. The now familiar and symbolic string of beads and knotted cord were adopted simply as counting aids.

The word *rosary* means "crown of roses" (from the Latin *rosarium* or "rose garden"). The symbolism stems from the custom of offering spiritual bouquets—gifts of prayers—in

143

honor of other believers. The rose is also one of the early symbols of the Virgin Mary. The rosary combines a long series of invocations to the mother of our Lord, held together by a scene from the life of Jesus or Mary, on which one meditates while saying the prayers. In my adult life, the rosary has become for me both a meditative tool and a form of intercessory prayer. I have learned to recognize those moments when I'm lying in bed or taking a walk and someone specific comes to mind as the Holy Spirit's urging me to pray for that particular person. Whether or (more than likely) not I have time for the whole rosary or even follow the specific process of how to say the rosary, I take that opportunity to offer a decade of the rosary (set of ten Hail Marys) for the person I am thinking about. In this way, I bring that person into my prayer as I call God into my moment and my consciousness. It is my bouquet of prayers offered on their behalf.

Through the centuries, the religious exercise of reflecting on Scriptures has remained a meaningful form of prayer in the church. All the prayers of the rosary, as well as the fifteen familiar events in the lives of Jesus and Mary that serve as meditations for each decade, are found in the Scriptures. In three sets (joyful, sorrowful, and glorious) of five mysteries each, a person praying the rosary meditates through familiar stories on the Christian history of salvation, using a verse or two of Scripture at a time. In much the same way that a stained-glass window in a church invites us to dwell on God by presenting a moment in the life of Christ or

MARY IN PRAYER—POPULAR DEVOTION

a picture of a saint, the rosary uses our fingers and our lips to invite our hearts to recall and meditate on Scripture.

The mysteries meditated on in the rosary are divided in the following way. The Scripture verses that follow the mystery are usually read at the beginning of each decade.

The Joyful Mysteries

The Annunciation

> Upon arriving, the angel said to her: "Rejoice, O highly favored daughter! The Lord is with you. Blessed are you among women." (Luke 1:28)

The Visitation

> Elizabeth was filled with the Holy Spirit and cried out in a loud voice: "Blest are you among women and blest is the fruit of your womb." (Luke 1:41–42)

The nativity of Jesus

> She gave birth to her first-born son and wrapped him in swaddling clothes and laid him in a manger, because there was no room for them in the place where travelers lodged. (Luke 2:7)

The presentation of Jesus in the temple

> When the day came to purify them according to the law of Moses, the couple brought him up to Jerusalem

so that he could be presented to the Lord, for it is
written in the law of the Lord, "Every first-born male
shall be consecrated to the Lord." (Luke 2:22–23)

Finding the child Jesus in the temple

On the third day they came upon him in the temple
sitting in the midst of the teachers, listening to them
and asking them questions. (Luke 2:46)

The Sorrowful Mysteries

The agony in the Garden

In his anguish he prayed with all the greater intensity,
and his sweat became like drops of blood falling to the
ground. Then he rose from prayer and came to his
disciples, only to find them asleep, exhausted with
grief. (Luke 22:44–45)

The scourging at the pillar

Pilate's next move was to take Jesus and have him
scourged. (John 19:1)

The crowning with thorns

They stripped off his clothes and wrapped him in a
scarlet military cloak. Weaving a crown out of thorns

they fixed it on his head, and stuck a reed in his right hand. (Matthew 27:28–29)

The carrying of the cross

Jesus was led away, and carrying the cross by himself, went out to what is called the Place of the Skull (in Hebrew, *Golgotha*). (John 19:16–17)

The Crucifixion

Jesus uttered a loud cry and said,
"Father, into your hands, I commend my spirit."
After he said this, he expired. (Luke 23:46)

The Glorious Mysteries

The Resurrection

You need not be amazed! You are looking for Jesus of Nazareth, the one who was crucified. He has been raised up; he is not here. See the place where they laid him. (Mark 16:6)

The ascension of Jesus

No sooner had he said this than he was lifted up before their eyes in a cloud which took him from their sight. (Acts of the Apostles 1:9)

The descent of the Holy Spirit upon the apostles

> All were filled with the Holy Spirit. They began to
> express themselves in foreign tongues and make bold
> proclamations as the Spirit prompted them. (Acts of
> the Apostles 2:4)

The assumption of Mary into heaven

> A great sign appeared in the sky, a woman clothed with
> the sun, with the moon under her feet, and on her
> head a crown of twelve stars. (Revelation 12:1)

The coronation of the Blessed Virgin Mary

> You are the glory of Jerusalem,
>   the surpassing joy of Israel;
>   You are the splendid boast of our people. . . .
>   God is pleased with what you have wrought.
> May you be blessed by the Lord Almighty
>   forever and ever! (Judith 15:9–10)

The ordinary practice of praying the rosary calls for
meditation on one set of mysteries. Before each decade of Hail
Marys (there are five in the rosary), a mystery is announced and
then meditated on throughout that decade. The rosary begins
on the pendant with the sign of the cross and the recitation of
the Apostles' Creed on the crucifix. It continues with an Our
Father, three Hail Marys, the Doxology, and another Our
Father. Then follows the recitation of Hail Marys on the

decades of small beads, each decade separated from the next by a larger bead, on which an Our Father is recited and a new mystery is announced. Each decade of the rosary is preceded by the Gloria Patri, or the Doxology: "Glory to the Father, and to the Son, and to the Holy Spirit: as it was in the beginning, is now, and will be forever."

The evolution of the rosary's form and how it spread as a private devotion among believers is commonly associated with several saints. In the Western church, St. Bridget of Ireland (c. 450–525) used a rosary similar to the rosary we know today, made up of Hail Marys and Our Fathers. Historians believe it was an Irish monk who suggested to the people around his monastery that they pray a series of 150 Our Fathers in place of the 150 psalms of the Bible that the monks chanted. According to the online Catholic Encyclopedia, strings of beads have been discovered in the tomb of St. Rosalia (d. 1160).

Because the rosary as we know it developed over centuries, no one person can take credit for its invention. As I said earlier, because of the fact that the laity, including lay brothers, were often illiterate and could not follow the 150 psalms, the prayer they began to recite throughout the day was the Our Father—and the rosary was simply the tool they used to keep count of those prayers. Historical evidence supports the belief that by the eleventh and twelfth centuries, people were using pebbles, berries, and even disks of bone threaded on a string. Such "strings of beads," notes the

MARY IN PRAYER—POPULAR DEVOTION

online Catholic Encyclopedia, were known throughout the Middle Ages as "paternosters" (from the Latin for "Our Father," the Lord's Prayer). "Already in the thirteenth century the manufacturers of these articles, who were known as 'paternosterers,' almost everywhere formed a recognized craft guild of considerable importance. . . . Paternoster Row in London still preserves the memory of the street in which their English craft-fellows congregated." During the twelfth century, the practice of "saying" or "praying" the rosary began to include the first half of what we now know as the Hail Mary, with the second half being added years later.

St. Dominic de Guzman (1170–1221), founder of the Order of Preachers (the Dominicans) and a contemporary of St. Francis of Assisi, is popularly attributed with inventing the rosary in its current form. According to the story, St. Dominic received in a vision from the Blessed Mother the command to preach and to popularize this devotion for the prosperity of the church. Historians, however, point out that both the invention of the beads as a counting tool and the practice of repeating the 150 Hail Marys or Our Fathers cannot be credited to St. Dominic because they were in practice long before his time. But although the rosary doesn't owe its invention to Dominic, the sons and daughters of St. Dominic (the Dominican Order) have undoubtedly been the rosary's greatest promoters over the centuries.

The Order of Carthusians has also contributed greatly to the development of the rosary as we know it today. According to most sources, it was Dominic of Prussia, a Carthusian monk, who sometime between 1410 and 1439 linked fifty Hail Marys with fifty phrases referring to Jesus and Mary. And it was Henry of Kalkar, another Carthusian, who divided the fifty Hail Marys into decades, with an Our Father between each.

In 1569, the papal bull *Consueverunt Romani pontifices* officially established the devotion of the rosary in the church. In addition, saints such as Peter Canisius (1521–97) and Alphonsus Liguori (1696–1787), as well as popes from Leo XIII to John Paul II, have contributed significantly to the promotion of the rosary as a personal devotion.

The church tradition regards the process of meditation—engaging thought, imagination, emotion, and desire—as a necessary means to deepening our conviction of faith. To say or to pray the rosary is, ultimately, to take the time to meditate upon a particular mystery of our redemption and to learn to treasure it in our hearts, as Mary did when the events were actually taking place. Because of this, the rosary was called "an epitome of the whole Gospel" by Pope Paul VI.

"The beauty of the Rosary is that it is not merely a vocal prayer. It is also a mental prayer," wrote Archbishop Fulton J. Sheen. "One sometimes hears a dramatic presentation in which, while the human voice is speaking, there is a background of beautiful music, giving force and dignity to the words. The Rosary is like that. While the prayer is being said, the heart is not hearing music, but it is meditating on the life of Christ all

over again, applied to one's own life and one's own needs."
As Archbishop Sheen says, the rosary can help us to sanctify
all the idle moments of our lives. Taking a walk, driving in
the car, waiting for the subway or in line at the supermarket
all become opportunities to focus on God's presence with us
at that moment and to regain our spiritual centers. A few
years ago, my husband, Michael, started praying the rosary
on the twenty-five-minute drive to pick up our children from
school each day, a practice I have now adopted. When we do
this, the rosary becomes a prayer that helps us to follow Paul's
invitation to pray at all times and under all circumstances.

To say or to pray the rosary is, ultimately, to take the time to meditate upon a particular mystery of our redemption and to learn to
treasure it in our hearts, as Mary did when the events were actually
taking place.

In a practical and concrete way, the rosary can be a
useful, prayerful tool in our spiritual lives. By meditating on
each of the mysteries presented in the rosary, we are invited
to make a journey with Mary, the first Christian. As the
body of the faithful has proclaimed throughout the ages by
their lives and by their words, prayer is not doing but being.
In our connectedness with believers across time, we turn to
the example of those who came before us for encouragement
and direction. We use the church's body of formulated and

defined prayers as a tool to help us to be prayerful throughout our day. Through the rosary, Mary's life—her willingness to say yes to God's mystery of salvation—becomes for each of us a living sermon, a guide, and a sign.

The Angelus

The angel of the Lord declared unto Mary;
And she conceived of the Holy Spirit.
Hail Mary, full of grace . . .
Holy Mary, Mother of God . . .
Behold the handmaid of the Lord;
Be it done to me according to thy word.
Hail Mary, full of grace . . .
Holy Mary, Mother of God . . .
And the Word was made flesh;
And dwelt among us.
Hail Mary, full of grace . . .
Holy Mary, Mother of God . . .
Pray for us, O holy Mother of God,
That we may be worthy of the promises of Christ.
Let us pray.

Pour forth, we beseech you, O Lord, your grace into our hearts, that we to whom the incarnation of Christ, your Son, was made known by the message of an angel, may, by his passion and cross, be brought to the

153

glory of his resurrection, through the same Christ our Lord. Amen.

The devotion known as the Angelus, a prayer commemorating the incarnation of Jesus, is named for its first Latin words: *Angelus Domini*, "Angel of the Lord." The Angelus consists of three versicles, three Hail Marys, and a special prayer. The words recited recall the announcement to Mary by the archangel Gabriel that she was chosen to be the mother of Christ, as well as her acceptance of the divine will and the Incarnation, all of which are taken from the Gospel of Luke.

The origin of this prayer is unknown, though it may date back as far as the tenth century. Historians seem to agree that the practice began with the tolling of monastery bells for compline or curfew. According to the *Our Sunday Visitor's 2000 Catholic Almanac*, the practice of reciting the Hail Mary in honor of the Incarnation was introduced by the Franciscans in 1263. Beginning in the sixteenth century, the bells of the local church or chapel rang the pattern of the Angelus as we now know it three times a day: at 6:00 A.M., at noon, and at 6:00 P.M. As the bells tolled, all within hearing—whether they were tilling fields, bridling horses, or making shoes—would stop and join the rest of the community in prayer.

In some parts of the world, such as some predominantly Catholic towns in Europe, the ringing of the local church bells continues, calling all within earshot to stop their

154

activities and recite the Angelus three times a day. In some Catholic schools and universities in the United States, saying the Angelus at noon remains a communal form of prayer. For most of us, however, because of our secular work settings and urban occupations, the recitation of the Angelus has become a strictly personal and private affair.

Salve Regina

Hail, holy Queen, Mother of mercy,
hail, our life, our sweetness, and our hope.
To you we cry, the children of Eve;
to you we send up our sighs,
mourning and weeping in this land of exile.
Turn, then, most gracious advocate,
your eyes of mercy toward us;
lead us home at last
and show us the blessed fruit of your womb, Jesus:
O clement, O loving, O sweet Virgin Mary.
Amen.

Perhaps the second most commonly recited prayer in praise of Mary (after the Hail Mary) is the Salve Regina, Latin for "Hail, Holy Queen," a prayer that dates back to approximately the eleventh century. The Salve Regina is a prayer of communal intercession that recalls the history of salvation and Mary's unique and merciful place in it: because

MARY IN PRAYER—POPULAR DEVOTION

of original sin, we are the poor banished children of Eve; we mourn and weep in the exile that is life on this earth, and we long to join Mary and her Son in heaven. This poetic prayer, often sung rather than recited, is a community's petition to Mary, our heavenly mother, that she ask God for the blessings and grace we need now so that we may one day see, through her, the blessed fruit of her womb, Jesus.

Although attributed to several authors, the Salve Regina was probably composed by Hermann of Reichenau (d. 1054). Its use at compline, the church's liturgical night prayer, was begun by the Dominicans around 1221 and spread rapidly. Eventually, the laity joined the monks and friars in singing it at the end of the day. It was incorporated, with other anthems of the Blessed Virgin, into the Franciscan breviary by the middle of the twelfth century, when it was also entered officially into the Roman breviary.

While the Salve Regina has been a popular hymn of praise in both liturgical and general Catholic devotion, according to the *Catholic Encyclopedia*, the hymn was especially dear to sailors. According to scholars, the sailors of Columbus's expeditions sang the Salve Regina.

Memorare

Remember, most loving Virgin Mary,
never was it heard

Gentlest of the gentle!
Chaste and gentle make us.
Still as on we journey,
Help our weak endeavor,
Till with you and Jesus
We rejoice forever.
Through the highest heaven,
To the Almighty Three,
Father, Son, and Spirit,
One same glory be.

The Latin version of this anonymous hymn in honor of the Virgin Mary—Ave, Maris stella—can be traced to the late eighth or early ninth century. It was widely popular in the Middle Ages and is still used in Marian Offices. The title used for Mary in the prayer, "Star of Ocean (or Sea)," is one of the oldest and most widespread titles for Mary.

The Ave, Maris stella is a beautiful poem that uses common and easily understood images of creation: the light of a star shining brightly over the ocean water, light in darkness, the devoted love of a human mother. Recalling Mary's role in the story of the Incarnation, the poem acknowledges Mary's yes to the angel Gabriel's hail, and it requests that she bring to her Son our sighs and petitions. Since Mary herself is a sign of hope for a safe arrival to one's destination, the prayer is often used to pray for travelers.

Antiphon in Honor of the Blessed Virgin

(recited following night prayer in the Liturgy of the Hours)

> Loving mother of the Redeemer,
> gate of heaven, star of the sea,
> assist your people who have fallen yet strive to rise again.
> To the wonderment of nature you bore your Creator,
> yet remained a virgin after as before.
> You who received Gabriel's joyful greeting,
> have pity on us poor sinners.

"To the wonderment of nature"—these words of the Antiphon in Honor of the Blessed Virgin, remarked Pope John Paul II in *Redemptoris Mater*, express that "wonderment of faith which accompanies the mystery of Mary's divine motherhood." At the center of this mystery, in the midst of this wonder of faith, stands Mary of Nazareth. As the mother of the Redeemer, she was the first to experience the mystery of the Incarnation: "To the wonderment of nature you bore your Creator." But it is a mystery that each of us is asked to personally ponder, meditate upon, and ultimately believe. It is the heart of our faith. Through this prayer, we request Mary's merciful assistance as the star of the sea in guiding us toward her Son, our final destination.

Through the rosary, Mary's life—her willingness to say yes to God's mystery of salvation—becomes for each of us a living sermon, a guide, and a sign.

One Final Word

"We do not go to Mary as our God, but we go to God through Mary, as faith tells us He came to us through her," wrote Fr. William Joseph Chaminade (1761–1850), founder of the Daughters of Mary Immaculate (1816) and the Society of Mary (1817). Mary, the mother of God, the mother of the church, continues from heaven to love and care for each of us as her children. In the way that only a mother can, our mother in heaven is close by and available, waiting to assist us and to guide us in our earthly and spiritual journey to her Son, Jesus. Marian devotions and prayers of petition have been used by the body of believers since the beginning of the church. The first Christians recognized the treasure available to us in the one who was human like us, yet became a vessel for God incarnate.

This motherhood of Mary in the order of grace continues uninterruptedly from the consent which she loyally gave at the Annunciation and which she sustained without wavering beneath the cross, until the eternal fulfillment of all the elect. . . . Therefore the Blessed Virgin is invoked in the Church under the

titles of Advocate, Helper, Benefactress, and Mediatrix.
(Catechism, 969)

These names, however, "are to be so understood that they neither take away nor add anything to the dignity and efficacy of Christ the one Mediator," declared the documents of the Second Vatican Council. In this manner, the church continues to profess Mary's subordinate role to that of her Son while reminding believers of the unique gift available to us in Mary's maternal help and intercession.

Mary, my dearest mother,
Give me your heart
So beautiful, so pure, so
Immaculate, so full of love
And humility, that I may
Receive Jesus as you did—
And go in haste to give him
To others.

—*MOTHER TERESA OF CALCUTTA*

CHAPTER SEVEN

Mary as Patron

One Person, Many Roles

I love to walk on the beach collecting shells. I love their rainbow of colors, their linear, oval, and unusual shapes. I love to give them names that simply resemble what I see, such as angel wings, the name I have given to the two conchlike shells that are still joined together when I find them at the surf line. Because I love to collect shells no matter what beach or coast I find myself on, a friend once gave me an official shell book that defines common shells by family and category. From the Peterson Field Guide Shell Book, I learned that there is a delicate type of shell called an angel wing, typically found buried in the mudflats, yet this is a completely different type of shell than the one I have always called angel wings.

It turns out that whether it is still joined or not, my angel wings shell is called Atlantic coquina. I have learned that, for me, knowing names such as pear whelk, yellow cockle, or scotch bonnet does not enhance my ability to enjoy collecting shells. I am aware that there are hundreds of families and species of shells, and I love wondering about the creature that inhabited the shell before I found it discarded on the beach. But the truth is that I don't need to know the shell's scientific name or its identifying marks to enjoy it. I don't need to know its dimensions or where it is likely to be found on the beach in order to appreciate it.

As have the hundreds of types of shells that exist in our oceans, the Virgin Mary has been given many names over time and across cultures, each representing the way that she has been present to a particular ethnic or cultural community or to a specific individual. Throughout history and across the globe, stories of Marian visitations to ordinary people have been told and retold from generation to generation. Each story names Mary in a way that is in keeping with a particular apparition to a specific community of people. By this process, Mary is also often named as the patroness of a country or a group of people. The Virgin Mary, for example, is known and venerated under the patron names of Our Lady of Luján in Argentina and Uruguay, the Immaculate Conception in Portugal, Our Lady of Charity in Cuba, Our Lady of Sorrows in Ecuador and Slovakia, and Our Lady of the Assumption in India and Paraguay.

There is only one Virgin Mary, one Mary of Nazareth, who gave birth to Jesus the Christ approximately two thousand years ago. Yet each story of how our Lady spoke to a particular group of people, such as the story of the olive-skinned Lady of Guadalupe who visited the Aztec Indian Juan Diego, reflects both Mary's ability to be present in a personal way to the experience of a particular person or group and her universality as mother of God and mother of us all, across time and cultures. Like a finely tuned instrument playing in a delicate symphony, Mary is attuned to the needs, desires, and lived experiences of every community in the world. This is the case whether or not Mary's appearances to them have been recognized by the Catholic Church as official Marian apparitions.

Whether I, as an amateur shell collector, call a certain shell I find on the beach angel wings or define it by its common name as Atlantic coquina, the shell remains the same. And while I always remain the same person, I am variously known as a mother, a daughter, a wife, a sister, a friend, an RCIA sponsor, a writer, a woman, a granddaughter, a eucharistic minister, an aunt, and a Cuban-born American. In much the same way, the various names of the Virgin Mary describe both her spiritual dimensions and the personal ways in which she has touched the lives of her children throughout history. Some of her titles describe her nature: Our Lady of Sorrows, Our Lady Queen of Peace, Mother of Mercy, Our Lady of Hope, Our Lady of the Immaculate Conception, Our Lady of Consolation. Other names are connected with specific sites of apparitions or miracles: Our Lady of Lourdes,

Our Lady of Beauraing, Our Lady of La Salette (France), Our Lady of Guadalupe.

As have the hundreds of types of shells that exist in our oceans, the Virgin Mary has been given many names over time and across cultures, each representing the way that she has been present to a particular ethnic or cultural community or to a specific individual.

Mary: Patron of All

The hundreds of stories of apparitions by the Virgin Mary to a particular ethnic group or culture who have claimed her as patron are as varied and personal as the number of languages in the world. As the documents of the Second Vatican Council note, while the church has endorsed many forms of piety toward Mary, "these forms have varied according to the circumstances of time and place, and have reflected the diversity of native characteristics and temperament among the faith. While honoring Christ's Mother, these devotions cause her Son to be rightly known, loved and glorified, and all his commands observed. Through him all things have their beginning (Colossians 1:15–16) and in him 'it has pleased (the eternal Father) that all his fullness should dwell' (Colossians 1:19)."

The word *patron*, or *patroness*, refers to a sponsor or benefactor, one who supports, protects, or champions someone or something. Whether or not they are called patrons, mothers

that anyone who turned to you for help
was left unaided.

Inspired by this confidence,
though burdened by my sins,
I run to your protection
for you are my mother.

Mother of the Word of God,
do not despise my words of pleading
but be merciful and hear my prayer.
Amen.

The Memorare is a prayer that requests Mary's
intercession. It appears in texts as early as the fifteenth
century; its title, from the Latin, means "to call to mind." As
the words indicate, the person reciting the Memorare first
seeks, quite literally, to recall in Mary's mind and heart her
role as mother of all believers. Like a child attempting to
remind his mother that he is aware of and thankful for his
mother's devotion and love before he asks for a favor, the
Memorare begins by outlining the spiritual history of Mary's
relationship with Christian believers: you have been our
protector; you have asked for help on our behalf; you have
always interceded for believers in need. With this in mind,
the second part of the Memorare is the prayer of one who is
aware of his or her sin and unworthiness and humbly seeks
the mother's mercy, prayers, and intercession.

The Memorare is traditionally attributed to St. Bernard of Clairvaux (1090–1153), probably because Claude Bernard, the "Poor Priest" (1588–1641), popularized the idea of St. Bernard's authorship. The use of the prayer as a devotional prayer was promoted by Pope Pius IX.

Hail, You Star of Ocean

Hail, you Star of Ocean!
Portal of the sky,
Ever Virgin Mother,
Of the Lord most high.
O! by Gabriel's Ave,
Uttered long ago,
Eva's name reversing,
Establish peace below.
Break the captive's fetters;
Light on blindness pour;
All our ills excelling,
Ev'ry bliss implore.
Show yourself a mother;
Offer him our sighs,
Who for us Incarnate
Did not you despise.
Virgin of all virgins!
To your shelter take us;

There I knelt before the patroness of the Cuban people, Our Lady of Charity of El Cobre. I noticed with deep joy and emotion how much Cubans love the Mother of God, and how Our Lady of Charity is truly, over and above every difference, the principal symbol and support of the Cuban people's faith and their struggle for freedom. In this setting of popular piety, I urged them to incarnate the Gospel, the message of authentic liberation, in their daily lives by living as Christians fully involved in society. . . . I have entrusted to her care all Cubans, in their homeland and abroad, so that they may form a truly prosperous and fraternal community more and more enlivened by authentic freedom.

A similar visitation by Mary took place in Bolivia, near the Peruvian border. In the mountains near Lake Titicaca stand the ruins of an Incan temple dedicated to the god of the sun. This is also the site of a small shrine to the Virgin Mary that was built in 1583. It stands on the site where Incan fishermen, caught in a storm, were led to safety by the Virgin Mary, who was carrying the infant Jesus in her arms. The shrine holds the four-foot statue of la Virgen de la Candelaria, Our Lady of Copacabaña, a figure carved out of wood that over time was adorned with embroidered robes. Every year in mid-August, a replica of la Virgen de la Candelaria, patroness of Bolivia, is brought to the harbors to bless the boats and the fishermen.

MARY AS PATRON

Hundreds of years earlier and across the globe from Lake Titicaca, an Austrian Benedictine monk named Magnus decided in 1157 to retire from his abbey in order to follow a strict contemplative life in the wilderness. Legend has it that Magnus carried with him on his journey a small wooden statue of the Virgin and Jesus. When Magnus became lost in the deep woods, he prayed for Mary's intervention and, miraculously, a boulder blocking his way split in half and trees fell to give way to a clear path. In thanksgiving for his safety and protection, Magnus perched the statue in a tree, where it became a rustic shrine for pilgrims. One hundred years later, an Austrian prince and his wife became mortally ill. In a dream, the couple was told to seek out the statue left behind by Magnus. They visited the shrine, and both were miraculously cured. In thanksgiving, the prince and his wife built a church that later acquired a monastery and became known as Mariazell, or Mary's cell. After that, Our Lady of Mariazell—now residing in a lavish golden chapel—became the patron of successive queens and kings of the Hapsburg dynasty, who asked for her advice and intercession.

In England, one of the most famous and popular shrines to Mary was built in the Norfolk countryside in 1061 by a pious noblewoman named Richeldis de Faverches, who said that Mary had commanded her to build a replica of Mary's holy house in Nazareth. What became known as the shrine to Our Lady of Walsingham was soon an important pilgrimage site, a place of healing and miraculous interventions. By the middle of the thirteenth century, however, the once humble chapel had been incorporated into a great church, crowned with towers and given a magnificent high altar. The church was destroyed and the original statue of the Virgin was burned in 1538 following Henry VIII's break from the Catholic Church. In 1897, the church was bought by a Catholic and restored.

During his first visit to Poland as pope in 1979, John Paul II prayed before the Black Madonna known as Our Lady of Czestochowa, the patron of his home country. Sometimes called Our Lady of Jasna Gora after the monastery site in which it has been kept for six centuries, the Black Madonna of Czestochowa is among the most recognized statues of Mary throughout the world, largely because of the public piety shown by our reigning Polish pope.

According to the Marian Library, Our Lady of Czestochowa's image is so old that its origins are unknown, "as if [it] dropped from the heavens." Legend attributes its creation to St. Luke the Evangelist, who is said to have painted a portrait of the Virgin on the cedarwood table at which she ate. According to the legend, St. Helena, the queen mother of the emperor Constantine, located this portrait during her visit to the Holy Land and took it to Constantinople in the fourth century. After remaining there for five centuries, the portrait was apparently transferred in royal dowries until it made its way to Poland and to St. Ladislaus in the fifteenth century. The legend states that during Ladislaus's time, the

MARY AS PATRON

image was damaged by a Tartar arrow during a siege, inflicting a scar on the throat of the Blessed Virgin.

It is said that in 1430, Hussites stole and vandalized the precious image, breaking it into three pieces. One of the robbers even made two deep gashes in the image with his sword. While preparing to inflict a third gash, however, he fell to the ground and squirmed in agony until he died. As the legend notes, the two slashes on the cheek of the Blessed Virgin and the scar on the throat have always reappeared despite repeated attempts to repair them. The miracles worked by Our Lady of Czestochowa seem to have occurred on a public scale. According to legend, the image frightened the besieging Saracens away from Constantinople, and in 1655, our Lady was credited with helping a small group of Polish defenders drive off from its sanctuary a much larger army of Swedish invaders. The following year, King Casimir proclaimed Our Lady of Czestochowa the queen of Poland.

During his reign as pope, John Paul II returned to his native Poland in 1983 and again in 1991 to pray before Our Lady of Czestochowa.

One with Her People

Religion, culture, faith, and values are inseparable for a people, and the Catholic Church respects the intricate connection between a particular culture and its personal expression of the truths of the gospel. While the Incarnation was God's revelation in its fullness, God has continued to speak to people according to their culture and experience. God is not confined to one ethnicity, to one period in history, or to one region of the world. God continues to reveal God's love to us through the variety of people and things God has made. In much the same way, the catholic church, the universal church, has existed in a variety of manifestations through the centuries. In our world, it is essential to proclaim the Good News with an awareness that respects diversity and native-ethnic individuality in the Christian community. There is no greater instrument for this expression than Mary.

Devotion and veneration to Mary are integral parts of the Catholic faith as lived out by the Hispanic people, and this is also true for many other ethnic groups. As did the first Christians, Hispanics find it natural to turn to Mary as their mother, seeking her protection and asking for her intercession on their behalf. The Latin American Bishops' Conference (CELAM) has consistently pointed out, for example, that Marian shrines in the American continent, such as the one in honor of Our Lady of Guadalupe outside Mexico City, are explicit signs of the encounter between Latin American history and the faith of the people of God, the living church.

For many of the Hispanic ethnic groups, in fact, Marian piety has been the enduring bond that has maintained the people's fidelity to the church. This connection to Mary is at times the only link that remains between simple believers and the life of the church. Yet this connection, if a true one, can

MARY AS PATRON

be Mary's ultimate gift to her Son's church on earth. Through Mary, those who have become distant from Jesus and the expression of their faith can be born anew. A good example in recent history has taken place in Cuba, one of the most persecuted churches in modern times because of Fidel Castro's openly hostile attitude toward religion. In spite of decades of religious oppression and persecution, Our Lady of Charity remains a symbol of a faith that cannot be suppressed. In preparation for Pope John Paul II's 1998 trip to this island nation, the bishops of Cuba arranged for the original image of Nuestra Señora de la Caridad to travel the island from one end to the other, with public processions and Masses in as many towns as the government would allow. Even the church was surprised by the outcome.

"While it's not strange, the reaction to Our Lady was a surprise," noted the bishop of Pinar del Río, José Ciro Gonzalez, during the pope's visit. "We did not anticipate such a reaction. The love for the Virgin Mary is incredible. Young mothers take their children to her so they may kiss her, they take them to her carrying flowers—as it once was at one time long ago with their grandparents and parents," explained the bishop, noting that forty years of Communist rule have left the people obviously lacking in formal religious instruction. "This spontaneous devotion to *la virgencita* fills us not only with enthusiasm but with a song of joy for God who brings these things to pass after almost forty years. It's a miracle brought forth by the hand of God."

It is essential to proclaim the Good News with an awareness that respects diversity and native-ethnic individuality in the Christian community. There is no greater instrument for this expression than Mary.

On Shrines and Pilgrimages

The church has always regarded shrines as important in Christian life, and the twenty-four-page document on the significance of shrines, produced in 1999 by the Pontifical Council for the Pastoral Care of Migrants and Itinerant People, reiterates this idea. The document highlights the importance of three distinct aspects of shrines. First, they not only remind us of God's powerful activity in history but also point to his constant presence and invitation for all to share in his love. Second, they help us to discern the goal of our lifelong pilgrimage. And third, Marian shrines in particular "provide an authentic school of faith based on Mary's example and motherly intercession."

More than buildings or impressive structures, shrines are "oases of the spirit," said John Paul II. They offer the Christian community ideal settings for meditating on the Word of God and for celebrating the sacraments, particularly the sacrament of reconciliation and the Eucharist. Ideally, shrines are places where Christian believers revive their faith and where they go to become more deeply aware of the duties and responsibilities that arise from that faith and its expression.

A shrine can be a church or another sacred place visited by believers who are pilgrims for special devotion. In Italy, at the first meeting of rectors of Marian shrines, Pope Paul VI urged the rectors to "lift their voices and let their existence be known in the Church." Noted Marianist Brother John M. Samaha observed that in the annual addresses to these rectors

> Paul VI was concerned with the meaning of shrines and their place in the liturgical and pastoral life of the Church. He described shrines as "spiritual clinics" (1965), "testimonies of miraculous deeds and of a continual wave of devotion" (1966), "luminous stars in the Church's sky, . . . centers of devotion, of prayer, of recollection, of spiritual refreshment" (1970). He recommended that shrines have a full program of sacramental and pastoral activity, and that they be centers of genuine religious intensity. He made it clear that devotion is an extension of liturgy and a preparation for it, that all Christian worship leads to Christ.

During the Jubilee Year 2000, our family had the unique opportunity to travel to Europe for an extended summer visit. Even during the planning stages, we were aware that this would be the trip of a lifetime. We visited cathedrals and shrines in small towns and large cities, from Rome and Assisi to Salzburg, Köln, Paris, and London, our family of two adults and four teens entering churches together and praying under the Jubilee Year banner. In the hometown of St. Francis of Assisi, we heard people speaking English and realized that a Mass was just beginning in one of the chapels of the centuries-old cathedral. With delight, we enjoyed beautiful hymns sung by an American high school choir that was also on a pilgrimage.

After Mass, our family divided into three sets of two to stand in lines to celebrate the sacrament of reconciliation in the language of our choice. Over and over, we were moved by the faith of the pilgrims present and by the unity that bound our faith together across races, nationalities, and languages. We found that the buildings themselves bore witness to the faith of those who had built them as their own form of prayer. These structures also served as reminders that our God has been present throughout all of history, in every culture and nation. The universality of our faith has never been more profoundly evident to me. It was a pilgrimage that transformed my life, and I pray that it will remain alive in my children's memories forever.

The concept of pilgrimage is prominent in all of the major world religions—Christianity, Judaism, Islam, Hinduism, Buddhism. In the Christian church, pilgrimage is an ancient custom with deep spiritual meaning. The early medieval period was a time when pilgrimages were encouraged—to Jerusalem; to the tombs of the apostles, saints, and martyrs; to the holy places of Rome; and to churches and shrines holding relics of saints. Not meant to be sightseeing trips or vacations, pilgrimages to sacred places honoring a significant person or event in Christian history—whether undertaken alone, as a family, or as a faith community—are meant to evoke the believer's personal journey with Jesus.

In the Catholic world, about 80 percent of all shrines are dedicated to Mary, and the vast majority of pilgrims are destined for them. Ten million go to Guadalupe in Mexico each year, five million go to Lourdes in France, five million to Czestochowa in Poland, and four million to Aparecida in Brazil. All of these sites of Marian apparitions have become noted centers of prayer and renewal.

Two things became immediately clear to us upon our family's arrival at Lourdes. First, one has to plan to go to Lourdes. This small town in southwestern France is not necessarily a good tourist stop on the way to another site; it is a place for pilgrims. And second, Lourdes is a wonderful symbol of our universal faith. The story of the young Bernadette brings together pilgrims of all cultures, all social and economic classes, all languages, all colors, all ages, and both genders. Inspired by the spirit and faith of seers such as Bernadette, pilgrims come to the grotto seeking spiritual courage, physical healing, or the grace to open themselves in new ways to God's presence in their lives.

MARY AS PATRON

Everything about a pilgrimage—the spiritual preparation leading to the journey, the vigils and prayers at the shrine, the celebration of the Eucharist at the sanctuary, the return home—is meant to be both symbolic and spiritually transforming. For our family of six, the opportunity to celebrate a multilingual Sunday Mass in the underground basilica at Lourdes was a very moving experience. As we received the Eucharist that day, we embodied the reality and gift of the universal Body of Christ. Our different languages did not matter. Our different cultures did not matter. Our countries' histories, governments, and the socioeconomic classes of those present did not matter. We were all branches of the true vine, and that was all that mattered.

In this way, Marian shrines often become centers of evangelization. "Even in the Church today, as in the community awaiting Pentecost, prayer with Mary spurs many Christians to the apostolate and to the service of their brothers and sisters," the pope remarked in 1995. "Encouraged by Mary's presence, believers have often felt the need to dedicate themselves to the poor, the unfortunate and the sick, in order to be for the lowliest of the earth a sign of the motherly protection of the Blessed Virgin, the living icon of the Father's mercy."

As magnificent as the great cathedrals that formed the world's first skylines are, it has been the small shrines and churches dedicated to Mary that have best spoken of the natural relationship between Mary and the body of believers.

These places of pilgrimage, where believers go to seek refuge from trials and hardships and to give thanks, are "centers of deep Marian spirituality, [where] people learn to grow in faith and in the desire to imitate Our Lady in purity and in humble submission to God's will," the pope said in his address to the rectors of shrines. "Mary leads us to Christ, in whom the human family is called to become the family of God's children."

In a very real way, the hospitality extended to migrants and to all pilgrims at these Marian shrines is a symbolic expression of Mary's welcoming of the Word's becoming flesh within her womb. Shrines can be unique places of welcome to visitors and especially to persons whom life has treated harshly, such as the poor, the sick, and those who are distant from the church. They can provide each of us, as pilgrims, with a vision of the loving hospitality with which God calls us to live as individuals and as communities. In this way, we are not only evangelized by our visit, but when we go home to our individual countries and cities, we also become the evangelizers.

The Basilica of the National Shrine of the Immaculate Conception, Washington, D.C.

Thousands of pilgrims journey each year from every state and from many foreign lands to the Basilica of the Immaculate Conception, in our nation's capital. This magnificent basilica is located on the southwestern corner of the campus of the Catholic University of America, and it

MARY AS PATRON

offers a unique visual representation of twentieth-century Catholicism in the United States. Designated as a minor basilica by Pope John Paul II in 1990, the Basilica of the Immaculate Conception remains a national symbol of Catholic devotion to Mary. Like the medieval cathedrals built centuries ago, this Washington, D.C., shrine—the largest Catholic church in the Western Hemisphere and the eighth largest in the world—is constructed entirely of stone.

This national shrine is the United States's "Patronal Church." In 1847, seven years before the proclamation of the dogma of the Immaculate Conception, Pope Pius IX proclaimed Mary "Patroness of the United States." By the early 1900s, Bishop Thomas J. Shahan, fourth rector of the Catholic University of America, proposed building a national shrine in Washington to honor Mary. As Bishop Shahan wrote in the inaugural issue of the shrine's newsletter in 1914, the Shrine of the Immaculate Conception is "a monument of love and gratitude, a great hymn in stone . . . as perfect as the art of man can make it and as holy as the intentions of its builders could wish it to be."

In the 1999 fall/winter issue of the shrine's newsletter, the shrine's rector, Monsignor Michael J. Bransfield, recalled that to help build the shrine,

> generations of American Catholics rallied to the cause contributing in ways both great and small, ultimately ensuring that this resplendent church would forever

183

symbolize the monumental accomplishments of the
Catholic Faith in the United States. That Bishop
Shahan's plans for establishing the National Shrine
prevailed despite two world wars and the Great
Depression, testifies to the truth of the Psalmist's
words that "unless the Lord build the house, in vain do
the builders labor" (Psalm 127:1).

Since its dedication on November 20, 1959, people have still
been working to complete this national shrine. Few then
could have envisioned the shrine as we know it today, with
its more than sixty chapels and oratories representing the
histories, struggles, and accomplishments of our nation's
diverse immigrant population. Our Lady of Czestochowa,
Queen of Peace, Our Mother of Sorrows—each chapel is
dedicated to the way in which Mary has been present to a
particular ethnic or cultural community. Though diverse,
the examples of Marian devotion at the Shrine of the
Immaculate Conception demonstrate, above all, the universal
nature of Mary's motherhood.

The Byzantine-Ruthenian Chapel, for example,
represents the Eastern Catholic churches. One of the shrine's
most popular Marian chapels is the one honoring Our Lady
of Guadalupe, the patroness of the Americas, often visited by
pilgrims from Mexico and from throughout Latin America.
Some of the shrine's other chapels, all of which host regular
devotions or Masses, include Our Lady of Perpetual Help

(Filipino community), Our Lady of Good Health (Vailankanni, Asian Indian community), Queen of Missions Chapel (Ugandan community), Chapel of Our Lady of Brezje (Slovenian community), Our Lady of Siluva (Lithuanian community), and the Mother of Africa Chapel (African American community).

As a symbol and as a site, the national shrine ultimately provides Catholics and other people of faith with a living reminder of Mary's faithful obedience to God. Each of the chapels represents a different Marian devotion, symbolizing the church's catholicity—its universal nature—and reminding visitors that despite the diverse ways in which Catholics from different cultures and countries honor her, Mary remains the mother of all, calling to unity all who are in the family of God.

From South America to Eastern Europe, from Africa to the Pacific Islands, devotion to Mary manifests itself in uniquely personal ways, showing the often striking cultural differences among Christians. The building of the National Shrine of the Immaculate Conception, with its dozens of ethnic representations housed under one roof, embodies the paradox revealed by Mary's motherhood to the community of believers: the universal church is experienced through our diversity.

> With the feet of a pilgrim
> We follow the Mother
> Of Christ, our Redeemer,

Our Savior, our Friend.
We walk a pathway,
Sinners and saints,
Through fields white for the harvest
To God's reign without end.

(Refrain)

With the heart of a pilgrim
We share with God's Mother
The hopes of a people
Longing for peace.
We treasure the mystery
Trust in the promise:
Behold the New City
Where joys never cease.

Refrain:
Mary, Mother of the Church,
Clothed, as with a robe, in light,
Lead us all, God's pilgrim people,
To the grace your Son has promised:
Hope fulfilled in vision,
Faith transformed in sight.
(Agnes Cunningham, S.S.C.M., "Pilgrim Hymn to
Mary")

Lord Jesus,

we gather in spirit at the foot of the Cross
with your Mother and the disciple whom you loved.
We ask your pardon for our sins
which are the cause of your death.
We thank you for remembering us
in that hour of salvation
and for giving us Mary as our Mother.
Holy Virgin,
take us under your protection
and open us to the action of the Holy Spirit.
Saint John,
obtain for us the grace of taking Mary
into our life, as you did,
and of assisting her in her mission. Amen.
May the Father and the Son
and the Holy Spirit
be glorified in all places
through the Immaculate Virgin Mary.

—*"THE THREE O'CLOCK PRAYER"*
Said around the world every day at 3:00 p.m. by members of the
Society of Mary

CHAPTER EIGHT

Mary in Today's Church

Human, Yet Full of Grace

In the long and shocking hours that followed the April 19, 1995, bombing of the Alfred P. Murrah building in Oklahoma City, hundreds gathered at the First Christian Church, just north of downtown. This was the official Red Cross center for family members awaiting news of their loved ones who were still unaccounted for. At first, rosters of names were posted hourly on the church's bulletin boards, listing the names of survivors and announcing the hospitals to which the injured had been taken. But as the hours turned into days and rescue efforts recovered bodies, the lists became shorter, less frequent, and more focused on the dead than on the living.

Of the many people I met and interviewed in my assignment as correspondent for the Catholic News Service during those traumatic days, the image of one young mother still haunts me. I spoke with Kathleen on the day following the disaster.

I can see her clearly in my memory. Kathleen had curly, brown, shoulder-length hair that was pulled back to reveal a tear-soaked, twenty-something woman's face. She had her arms crossed tightly, and she clutched a picture of her four-year-old daughter, Ashley, and Ashley's favorite stuffed animal. Ashley, one of the hundreds still unaccounted for on that day, had been with her grandparents on Wednesday, April 19, when they arrived at the Social Security office on the first floor of the Murrah building for a 9:00 A.M appointment. The bomb went off at 9:02.

"I am so very worried. I know her Nana wouldn't let anything happen to that baby girl," Kathleen said that night. "We believe in God," she paused, staring at nothing, "in spite of these monsters, these evil people, who are willing to hurt innocents who have never hurt anyone in their lives."

Standing silently next to his wife outside the Red Cross center, Kathleen's husband, Mike, kept his left hand firmly on her shoulder. As she answered the reporters' unending questions regarding her family, Kathleen struggled to get the words out. She simply wanted someone, anyone, to listen to her prayer that the rescue workers not give up. Her baby was in that mass of concrete and steel rubble and she had yet to be found.

"This was my baby," sobbed Kathleen, seemingly unaware of the contradiction in her words. "I still have hope that she's down there in a pocket somewhere. She's still missing. No one's found her. We are still waiting to know." She repeated these words like a mantra.

In the confusion and disorder that followed the bombing, several unidentified children and adults had been checked into area hospitals as John or Jane Doe. Aware of this fact, Kathleen held Ashley's picture up to the camera with a shaking hand and declared, "I want everyone to know what my little girl looks like in case they've seen her. If someone finds her, please bring her to me."

The young mother then added one final plea, both personal and global. Looking at the sea of reporters, she commented softly, "If we could just stop the killing and the hate, these senseless things wouldn't happen . . . oh, my baby. I just have to know. She was so very precious."

Four-and-a-half-year-old Ashley and her grandparents, LaRue and Luther Treanor, were eventually declared among the victims.

It is not difficult for me to find a connection between the image of this suffering mother and Mary at the Crucifixion, holding Jesus in her arms. Each of these mothers faced the unimaginable horror of having her precious child die at the hands of another human being. And even while lamenting the fact that a person could become so full of hate that he or she would transform into an evil monster, these women still turned to a God they knew in a personal and authentic way. They cried for their children—and yelled at

God in heaven—while at the same time continuing to believe in and affirm God's presence in their lives.

The words proclaimed by Kathleen on the night that followed the worst terrorist act on United States soil—"We believe in God"—echo perhaps the greatest and most profound profession of faith anyone can make. In spite of the pain that is piercing my heart; in spite of the knowledge that evil not only exists but, at times, suffocates the innocent; in spite of the fact that I would rather be dead myself than hold the dead body of the child whom I once bore within me; in spite of not understanding the mysterious reality unfolding in my life—I believe in God. It is a contradiction. It is a mystery. It is the ultimate act of faith.

This is Mary's gift to each one of us.

Mary of Nazareth is, undoubtedly, our greatest model in faith. She was the first Christian. She was the first to acknowledge that Jesus is the Son of the almighty God, the Messiah her Jewish people had long awaited. As the mother of God, the Blessed Virgin Mary holds a special and unequaled place in our faith. Mary participated in spirit in Christ's sacrifice on the cross, "lovingly consenting," as the pope has said, "to his sacrifice and offering her own sorrow to the Father." Every time we celebrate the Eucharist at Mass, "the memory of his Mother's suffering is also made alive and present, this Mother who, as an unsurpassable model, teaches the faithful to unite themselves more intimately to the sacrifice of her Son, the one Redeemer." Mary reigns in

MARY IN TODAY'S CHURCH

heaven and, from heaven, continues to intercede on our behalf. She is our heavenly mother.

Yet she is also a human mother like Kathleen, like me. She knows the joy and exhilaration of feeling new life move within her womb. She remembers the pain of childbirth, followed by the ecstasy of holding a miracle of life in her arms. She knows the delight of being able to feed a child from her breasts. Throughout her motherhood and her life, Mary worried, taught, loved, laughed, and gave of herself in a way that she would never have imagined possible. And, always, Mary treasured these things faithfully in her heart.

"Do Whatever He Tells You"

As my family and I walked through the main gate to the Lourdes sanctuary, it was clear to the six of us that we were entering a uniquely spiritual setting. Little did we know that, within minutes, we would naturally make the transition from spectators to full participants in this prayerful and spiritually enriching place.

There were lines of people everywhere. Many of the people were obviously sick, and they were always with helpers, who enabled them to take part in the ongoing liturgies and processions. There were vast numbers of young people all around us. Some were with youth groups that had traveled to Lourdes from one of the 170 countries represented there annually. For some, this was a first important stop before going to Rome to celebrate World Youth Day 2000. Many other children were among the workers, volunteers who had come to Lourdes for the express purpose of helping the sick and disabled. Those devoted to this work, whether nurses or volunteers, were easily recognizable. The men wore straps across their chests and the women wore white headdresses.

As if we had been there before, our family instinctively lined up to visit the Grotto of the Apparitions, to touch the rock where Mary long ago appeared and spoke to the young Bernadette. In silence, we touched the cold rock and the spring water flowing from it. Some people held hands, while others folded their own hands in prayer. Like petals making up the one rose, we stood with people of various nationalities, races, and languages and shared in the same faith. Old and young alike, many with rosary beads in hand, we stood or knelt in silence before the image of our Lady that has been placed at the grotto of Massabielle in the spot where Mary stood declaring to Bernadette, "I am the Immaculate Conception." One has to look up to see the statue of the apparitions. Perched on the rock and hanging from the rock itself are crutches, a testimony to the thousands of miracles and inexplicable cures that have taken place there since 1858. As had Bernadette before us, we lit a blessed candle and placed it in front of the grotto.

A pilgrimage to Lourdes or to any other Marian shrine means nothing if it doesn't in some way change the pilgrim.

Shrines are places where pilgrims are challenged to embrace repentance, discipleship, and a renewal of faith. As the sign above the water taps in Lourdes says, "Wash your face, drink this water and pray God to purify your heart." That is the gift of Marian apparitions, the legacy that Mary left behind. Her messages have often been simple and have always called the listener to prayer and to God. As she did to the waiters in Cana, Mary continues to command us as followers of Christ to "Do whatever he tells you" (John 2:5).

For centuries, the monarchical culture of Europe emphasized the divine interventions in Mary's life. As such, "Queen of Heaven" became Mary's most popular title, at the risk of presenting a picture of Mary as a Catholic pseudogoddess. This emphasis, however, seems contrary to the intimate relationship between Mary and her adopted children on earth that is implied in the messages she relayed in apparitions over the centuries: "Would you do me the kindness of coming here for fifteen days?" (to Bernadette at Lourdes); "Do not let anything afflict you and be not afraid. . . . Am I not here who am your mother?" (to Juan Diego at Tepeyac Hill); or "I come to alleviate suffering," "Believe in me, I will believe in you," and "Pray earnestly" (to Mariette at Banneux).

Rather than write a separate text on Mary, as had originally been planned, the bishops of the Second Vatican Council addressed the church's teaching on Mary as part of the Dogmatic Constitution on the Church (*Lumen Gentium*).

In chapter 8, "The Role of the Blessed Virgin Mary, Mother of God, in the Mystery of Christ and the Church," the church positions Mary historically in the midst of the pilgrim church and addresses her relationship to both Christ and the church. The final text achieves a delicate balance between the two historical tendencies regarding Mary, both of which have become extreme in the history of the church. On the one hand, Mary's unique connection with Christ the redeemer is emphasized, and on the other, the emphasis is on her close connection with the church and all the redeemed.

Mary is one with us in her humanity, and she accepts a singular function in the history of our salvation. It is in understanding the balance between her holiness and her humanity that Mary stops being just a theological issue and becomes someone with whom we are invited to have an intimate relationship.

Calling Mary "the privileged way to Christ, the supreme Mediator," Pope John Paul II remarked at a general audience on November 15, 1995, that the church's Marian dimension is an undeniable element in the experience of the Christian people. This Marian dimension is "not a superficial sentiment but a deep and conscious emotional bond, rooted in the faith which spurs Christians of the past and present to turn habitually to Mary, to enter into a more intimate communion with Christ." To honor Mary is to go to Jesus, the pope emphasized. "The Blessed Virgin is totally related to

Christ, the foundation of faith and ecclesial experience, and she leads to him."

A pilgrimage to Lourdes or to any other Marian shrine means nothing if it doesn't in some way change the pilgrim.

It is critical to center Marian theology on the knowledge of Mary as a woman of faith. As the first follower of Jesus, she is preeminent among the disciples, the first redeemed by and in Christ. Through both her Immaculate Conception and her assumption, she is also a symbolic embodiment of the ideal church, the first example of what the pilgrim people of God are destined to become. As Mary is now, in full communion with the God "who is mighty" and who "has done great things for [her]," we know we will one day also be.

Since the church's inception, Marian prayers, especially the Hail Mary, have been a part of the living tradition of the church and an authentic expression of faith as believers asked the holy mother of their Lord to guide and protect them on their daily journey through life. The counterpart of this Marian piety, the pope said in his 1995 remarks, is the rich and immense body of art that has enabled entire generations to appreciate Mary's spiritual beauty. "Painters, sculptors, musicians and poets have left us masterpieces which, in shedding light on the various aspects of the Blessed Virgin's greatness, help to give us a better understanding of the

MARY IN TODAY'S CHURCH

meaning and value of her lofty contribution to the work of Redemption."

Yet whether expressing our knowledge of Mary in art or in our lives, we must never steer our understanding and experience of Mary away from her humanity. We must continue to honor her unique role in salvation history. But we should also seek, in the awareness of her humanity, the example of a woman we can honestly emulate. And, just as the vast majority of artistic renditions of Mary show her accompanied by her Son, we are called to emulate a life with Christ and to heed her instruction to "Do whatever he tells you."

Mary in the Church Today—and Tomorrow

In the "Mailbag" section of the January 1, 2000, issue of *Time* magazine, a reader asked the following question: "Please, could you tell me which female has appeared on the cover more times than any other?" Although Queen Mary of England was the first to be pictured three times, the woman who has "turned up within the red border" the most times is Princess Diana, with nine covers. "Runner up is a tie, with eight covers apiece for both the Virgin Mary and Hillary Rodham Clinton (we aren't counting the tiny insert pics of Hillary on two Zippergate covers)," the editors explained. "But the race is not over. As campaign 2000 bears down upon us, we would have to say it's a reasonably good bet that the anticipated Democratic candidate for New York's U. S. Senate seat will go at least one up on the Virgin Mother and, if Hillary wins, may take the top spot away from Di. If that makes you queasy, rest easy," *Time* added. "It's nothing a religion cover or two won't cure."

It seems safe to predict that long after Princess Di and Hillary are forgotten, Mary will still be making the news—not bad for a humble and modest young woman from a small town named Nazareth.

"Once Marian imagery has truly been absorbed by a church or a culture, things are never simple. Or they are entirely so," remarks Kathleen Norris. "Who is this Mary? For one Benedictine sister, the biblical Mary exemplifies an intimate relationship to God, based on listening and responding to God's word, that 'calls Christians to the deep, personal, and daily love of Jesus Christ.' As for myself," writes the American poet from South Dakota,

> I have come to think of Mary as the patron saint of "both/and" passion over "either/or" reasoning, and as such, she delights my poetic soul. Ever since I first encountered Mary in that Benedictine abbey I have learned never to discount her ability to confront and disarm the polarities that so often bring human endeavors to impasse: the subjective and objective, the expansive and the parochial, the affective and the intellectual. . . . We could do worse than to stick with her, this Mary, who, as the affable parish priest in my

small town has said to me, has her ways of going in, under, around, and through any box we try to put her in.... There's a lot of *room* in Mary." (*Amazing Grace,* 121–23)

Indeed there *is* a lot of room in Mary. And this room is large enough and flexible enough for anyone, regardless of culture, ethnicity, or even religious background. As members of a church and faith that value the gifts of multiple cultures under one universal church, we honor Mary as a unique treasure. She is loved and venerated under many names and a myriad of images. But she is always the mother of God, the one who said yes to God's plan of salvation at the Annunciation. And she always points us to Jesus—through her life, through her words, and through our devotion to her.

In the words of Pope John Paul II (at the 1996 International Marian Congress in Czestochowa, Poland):

As we give thanks for 20 centuries of Mary's protection of the Church, let us together ask her to lead believers towards an ever more perfect knowledge of the saving power of the Sacrifice of Christ, who is present in the Eucharist. Let us pray that the living experience of communion with Christ may bear fruits of zeal in the hearts of all Christians as they build up a communion of love among men. May the Mother of God lead us into the third millennium, united around the Word of God who was made flesh in her.

Mary's love and concern for her children—across history and regardless of ethnicity or culture—seem to be what people of all generations treasure most about this Jewish woman. In the United States, Catholics can learn from their brothers and sisters in faith whose cultures are already aware of the gift available to all in Mary—their intercessor, protector, and mother. And they can grow in intimacy with the woman to whom other cultures—such as the various Asian and Hispanic communities—already turn in their grief and sorrow. The members of these communities already have a relationship with the heavenly mother, who understands anguish, joy, and sorrow and to whom they can relate as a person. And they are sure that this mother listens to them when they ask for her intercession. She is truly our mother, and she is waiting and ready to adopt and nurture each of us.

Mary's love and concern for her children—across history and regardless of ethnicity or culture—seem to be what people of all generations treasure most about this Jewish woman.

In recent years, as the Hispanic population in the United States has continued to grow, dioceses across the country have expanded their celebrations for December 12, the Feast of Our Lady of Guadalupe, patroness of the Americas. The following is the opening prayer of the memorial of Our Lady of Guadalupe:

MARY IN TODAY'S CHURCH

God of power and mercy,
you blessed the Americas at Tepeyac
with the presence of the Virgin Mary of Guadalupe.
May her prayers help all men and women
to accept each other as brothers and sisters.
Through your justice present in our hearts
may your peace reign in the world.
We ask this through our Lord Jesus Christ, your Son,
who lives and reigns with you and the Holy Spirit,
one God, for ever and ever.
Amen.

Let us embrace Our Lady of Guadalupe as patroness of *all* of the Americas. Let us hear and welcome the words that Mary first said to the Indian Juan Diego: "I am a merciful Mother, to you and to all your fellow men on this earth who love me and trust me and invoke my help." Let each of us, in a personal and communal way, allow the Blessed Lady of Tepeyac to teach us the mystery of the Incarnation so that Christ may be born in our hearts today and every day.

Oh! I would like to sing, *Mary, why I love you,*
Why your sweet name thrills my heart,
And why the thought of your supreme greatness
Could not bring fear to my soul.
If I gazed on you in your sublime glory,
Surpassing the splendor of all the blessed,
I could not believe that I am your child.

202

O Mary, before you I would lower my eyes! . . .

If a child is to cherish his mother,
She has to cry with him and share his sorrows.
O my dearest Mother, on this foreign shore
How many tears you shed to draw me to you! . . .
In pondering *your life in the holy Gospels,*
I dare look at you and come near you.
It's not difficult for me to believe I'm your child,
For I see you human and suffering like me. . . .

When an angel from Heaven bids you be *the Mother*
Of the God who is to reign for all eternity,
I see you prefer, O Mary, what a mystery!
The ineffable treasure of *virginity.*
O Immaculate Virgin, I understand how your soul
Is dearer to the Lord than his heavenly dwelling.
I understand how your soul, *Humble and Sweet Valley,*
Can contain Jesus, the Ocean of Love! . . .

Oh! I love you, Mary, saying you are the servant
Of the God whom you charm by your humility.
This hidden virtue makes you all-powerful.
It attracts *the Holy Trinity* into your heart.
Then *the Spirit of Love covering you with his shadow,*
The Son equal to the Father became incarnate in you,
There will be a great many of his sinner brothers,
Since he will be called: Jesus, your first-born! . . .

MARY IN TODAY'S CHURCH

O beloved Mother, despite my littleness,
Like you I possess The All-Powerful within me.
But I don't tremble in seeing my weakness:
The treasures of a mother belong to her child,
And I am your child, O my dearest Mother.
Aren't your virtues and your love mine too?
So when the white Host comes into my heart,
Jesus, your Sweet Lamb, thinks he is resting in you! . . .

You love us, Mary, as Jesus loves us,
And for us you accept being separated from Him.
To love is to give everything. It's to give oneself.
You wanted to prove this by remaining our support.
The Savior knew your immense tenderness.
He knew the secrets of your maternal heart.
Refuge of sinners, He leaves us to you
When He leaves the Cross to wait for us in Heaven.

Mary, at the top of Calvary standing beside the Cross
To me you seem like a priest at the altar,
Offering your beloved Jesus, the sweet Emmanuel,
To appease the Father's justice . . .
A prophet said, O afflicted Mother,
"There is no sorrow like your sorrow!"
O Queen of Martyrs, while remaining in exile
You lavish on us all the blood of your heart!

Saint John's home becomes your only refuge.

Zebedee's son is to replace Jesus. . . .
That is the last detail the Gospel gives.
It tells me nothing more of the Queen of Heaven.
But, O my dear Mother, doesn't its profound silence
Reveal that *The Eternal Word Himself*
Wants to sing the secrets of your life
To charm *your children,* all the Elect of Heaven?

Soon I'll hear that sweet harmony.
Soon I'll go to beautiful Heaven to see you.
You who came *to smile at me* in the morning of my life,
Come smile at me again . . . Mother. . . . It's evening
    now! . . .
I no longer fear the splendor of your supreme glory.
With you I've suffered, and now I want
To sing on your lap, Mary, why I love you,
And to go on saying that I am your child!
(St. Thérèse of Lisieux, from "Why I Love You, O
Mary!")

A Reader's Guide

This reader's guide provides discussion questions for each chapter of *The Seeker's Guide to Mary* and questions for reflection that address overarching ideas in the book. The format is simple and can be adapted to suit a variety of needs, time frames, and purposes.

- The questions can be used to discuss the book chapter by chapter, in sections, or as a whole, depending on whether you are holding brief weekly sessions or are meeting less frequently but for a longer period of time.

- Discussion and reflection can be limited to the questions provided or can be used to generate additional questions, according to the interests and goals of readers.

- This guide can be used by adult seekers in study groups, in high school faith-formation groups, or by individuals who are exploring aspects of the Catholic faith.

A Word to the Seeker: There's Something about Mary

María Ruiz Scaperlanda begins her introduction to Mary by describing the contrasting ways in which Mary has been presented: as an example of piety, trust, obedience, and faith, and as a strong, free, and intelligent woman; as a manifestation of radical feminism, and as a representation of the feminine power of God; as a point of division between Catholics and Protestants, and as central to the beliefs of all Christians. What is your understanding of Mary? How has this understanding developed through your life and been influenced by your faith tradition, your culture, your family?

Mary has been depicted by artists for centuries, and each has offered a unique representation of the mother of Jesus. Scaperlanda discusses the influence of Franco Zeffirelli's 1977 film, *Jesus of Nazareth,* on her personal image and understanding of Mary. Which, if any, artistic renditions of Mary have contributed to your image of her?

Scaperlanda identifies a key reason why we honor Mary and look to her for intercession when she says, "It is not only what sets Mary apart from us that makes her special, but also all that she has in common with each of us as a follower of Christ, as a woman, and as a mother." Is Mary a part of your personal prayer experience? If so, why do you turn to her with your prayers and petitions?

Chapter 1: Mary in Scripture

In this chapter, the author discusses how Mary's appearances in Scripture are important to our understanding of her. Scaperlanda says that "although Jesus' mother makes very few appearances in sacred Scripture, indications of Mary's special role in the life of Jesus and in our lives as a people of faith spring readily from the text." Which of Mary's roles in Scripture are you most drawn to?

- The courageous young teenager at the Annunciation?
- The new mother at the Nativity?
- The mother in political exile with her young family?
- The worried parent whose child is presumed lost?
- The confident woman at the wedding feast at Cana?
- The active, supportive first Christian in Jesus' ministry?
- The grieving mother at the Crucifixion?
- The disciple and apostle in the early church?

Why are you most drawn to this role?

Some people are troubled at first by the story of the wedding feast at Cana and the story of Jesus comparing his relationship with his followers to his relationship with his mother. Do any of the Scripture stories about Mary trouble you or challenge your faith?

Chapter 2: Mary, the First Christian

As the first person to say yes to Christ's presence in this world, likely amidst fear, anxiety, and confusion, Mary can be an example for us. The author describes a moment in which she recognized the Word's presence within her and said yes to

God in a unique and real way. Have you said yes in response to some call of God in your life?

Just as Mary's life was a series of yeses—to Christ being born in her, to her Son's death on the cross, to the Holy Spirit's presence at Pentecost—so must our lives as followers of Christ be experiences of saying yes daily. How can you continue to allow God to be born within you?

Discuss what it means to be both free and obedient, in light of Mary's life and actions.

Like Mary, who is our first example of faithfulness, St. Edith Stein is a modern example of one who lives a life of faith. Are there other people whose examples of faithfulness encourage you in your own faith journey?

Discuss the author's statement "As a church and as individuals, when we talk about Mary, we too often sound like teenagers embarrassed to be seen with their parents in public. We act as though talking about Mary is taking something away from Jesus, her Son."

Chapter 3: Mary in History

The author speaks of the importance of tradition in preserving and sustaining culture, both that of people and of the church. What are some of the traditions in your family? in your ethnic community? in your faith community?

Church tradition has played a significant role in the formation of our understanding of Mary and her life. As the church's understanding of Mary has grown and evolved, so has ours. What can you learn from the ways in which the church has struggled to define Mary's nature and roles at different times in its history?

One of Mary's most popular roles is that of intercessor. Just as we turn to friends and family to pray for us when we are in need, so can we ask Mary, our heavenly and spiritual mother, to intercede with God on our behalf. The author states that "this can easily become a vague theological concept unless we are able to place it within a human context." When have you experienced Mary's intercession? When have you experienced the intercession of a friend or family member?

Chapter 4: Mary in Other Faith Traditions

All Christians can agree that Mary is the mother of Jesus and thus is the spiritual mother of all Christians, yet, "in an unfortunate paradox caused by our human frailty, Mary has become a source of division among Christians, often widening the gap between Catholics and Protestants." What has been your experience of Mary? Is she a source of religious division? an expression of healthy diversity?

What are your personal beliefs about Mary's virginity? her immaculate conception? her role as mediator? her assumption? Do your views follow those of your faith tradition, or have you developed alternative ways of understanding these concepts?

Chapter 5: Mary in Her Apparitions

The opinion of our American culture seems divided over spiritual apparitions and interventions—we dismiss apparitions as hoaxes yet possess an obviously deep desire to understand the spiritual reality that surrounds us. What is your opinion regarding spiritual apparitions and interventions? With regard to this belief, do you feel that you are in the majority or the minority in your faith community?

In discussing the church's approach to apparitions of Mary, Scaperlanda explains, "When the church defines an apparition as 'worthy of belief,' a person is free to believe it or not. It is the believer's decision to accept or reject the reminder that its message conveys, which is always meant to bring attention back to faith in Christ." How do you feel about the stance of the Catholic Church that belief in approved apparitions is allowed but not required? Have you been influenced by stories you have heard about Mary's apparitions? If so, which stories appeal to you? Why do you think that is?

Chapter 6: Mary in Prayer—Popular Devotion

As a child, did you learn Marian prayers at school, at church, or at home? Did someone in your early life regularly pray the rosary or use some other form of Marian devotion? What impression did this make on you?

A READER'S GUIDE

According to Scaperlanda, for centuries the rosary has answered humans' instinctive desire to intertwine faith and life. Is this desire present in your life? Do you pray the rosary or any other Marian prayers as a regular part of your own religious practice? In what ways do you find them helpful? Are there any Marian prayers that don't work for you? Why don't they work?

Chapter 7: Mary as Patron

"The Virgin Mary has been given many names over time and across cultures, each representing the way that she has been present to a particular ethnic or cultural community or to a specific individual." Do you find these various representations helpful or detrimental to your understanding of Mary? Do the different cultural and religious views of Mary enrich your understanding or fragment it?

Is Mary the patron of some cause or community with which you are associated? How do you feel about this? Do you personally rely on Mary in some way?

Discuss the author's statement that "it is essential to proclaim the Good News with an awareness that respects diversity and native-ethnic individuality in the Christian community. There is no greater instrument for this expression than Mary."

Chapter 8: Mary in Today's Church

How would you describe your relationship with Mary? Are you satisfied with this relationship, or would you like to change it in some way? Has reading this book introduced you to aspects of Mary of which you were previously unaware? How will they affect your relationship with her?

The author explains that "a pilgrimage to Lourdes or to any other Marian shrine means nothing if it doesn't in some way change the pilgrim." For some, this book might have been a pilgrimage to a deeper understanding of Mary. Has your perception of Mary changed in reading this book? How so?

Mary's humanity must be central to our understanding of her. As Scaperlanda states, "It is in understanding the balance between her holiness and her humanity that Mary stops being just a theological issue and becomes someone with whom we are invited to have an intimate relationship." Do you experience Mary as present and active in your world, or do you consider her more of a legendary or historical figure? Are you satisfied with this experience? If not, how might what you have read here help you change it?

Selected Bibliography

Abbott, Walter M., S.J., ed. *The Documents of Vatican II.*
New York: Guild Press, 1966.

Dante Alighieri. *The* Paradiso *of Dante Alighieri.* London:
J. M. Dent and Co., 1904.

Ayo, Nicholas, C.S.C. *The Hail Mary: A Verbal Icon of Mary.*
Notre Dame, Ind.: University of Notre Dame Press,
1994.

Bettenson, Henry, ed. *Documents of the Christian Church.*
London: Oxford University Press, 1967.

Brown, Raymond E. *The Birth of the Messiah: A Commentary
on the Infancy Narratives in Matthew and Luke.* Garden
City, N.Y.: Doubleday, 1977.

Brown, Raymond E., et al., eds. *Mary in the New Testament:
A Collaborative Assessment by Protestant and Roman
Catholic Scholars.* Philadelphia: Fortress Press, 1978.

Bunson, Matthew, ed. *Our Sunday Visitor's 2000 Catholic
Almanac.* Huntington, Ind.: Our Sunday Visitor, 1999.

Cantalamessa, Raniero. *Mary: Mirror of the Church.* Trans.
Frances Lonergan Villa. Collegeville, Minn.: Liturgical
Press, 1992.

Catechism of the Catholic Church. Vatican City: Libreria
Editrice Vaticana, 1994.

Dickson, Charles. *A Protestant Pastor Looks at Mary.*
Huntington, Ind.: Our Sunday Visitor, 1996.

Dollen, Charles, ed. *Prayer Book of the Saints.*
Huntington, Ind.: Our Sunday Visitor, 1984.

Donne, John. *The Complete English Poems of John Donne.* Ed.
C. A. Patrides. London: Dent, 1985.

Donnelly, Doris. *Mary, Woman of Nazareth: Biblical and
Theological Perspectives.* New York: Paulist Press, 1989.

Gilles, Anthony E. *Fundamentalism: What Every Catholic
Needs to Know.* Cincinnati: St. Anthony Messenger
Press, 1984.

Jamart, François, O.C.D. *Complete Spiritual Doctrine of
St. Thérèse of Lisieux.* Trans. Walter Van de Putte.
New York: St. Paul Publications, 1961.

John of the Cross, St. *The Collected Works of St. John of the
Cross.* Trans. Kieran Kavanaugh, O.C.D., and Otilio
Rodriguez, O.C.D. Washington, D.C.: ICS, 1991.

The Liturgy of the Hours. New York: Catholic Book Publishing Co., 1975.

McBrien, Richard P., ed. *The HarperCollins Encyclopedia of Catholicism.* New York: HarperCollins, 1995.

McManus, Jim, C.Ss.R. *All Generations Will Call Me Blessed: Mary at the Millennium.* New York: Crossroad, 1999.

Norris, Kathleen. *Amazing Grace: A Vocabulary of Faith.* New York: Riverhead Books, 1998.

———. *Little Girls in Church.* Pittsburgh: University of Pittsburgh Press, 1995.

Rohr, Richard, and Joseph Martos. *Why Be Catholic? Understanding Our Experience and Tradition.* Cincinnati: St. Anthony Messenger Press, 1989.

Sheen, Fulton J. *The World's First Love: Mary, Mother of God.* San Francisco: Ignatius Press, 1996.

Staniforth, Maxwell, trans. *Early Christian Writings: The Apostolic Fathers.* Harmondsworth, U.K.: Penguin, 1968.

Stein, Edith. *An Edith Stein Daybook: To Live at the Hand of the Lord.* Trans. Susanne Batzdorff. Springfield, Ill.: Templegate Publishers, 1994.

————. *Essays on Woman.* Ed. L. Gebler and Romaeus Leuven, and trans. Freda Mary Oben. Washington, D.C.: ICS, 1996.

————. *Self-Portrait in Letters, 1916–1942: Edith Stein, Sister Teresa Benedicta of the Cross, Discalced Carmelite.* Trans. Josephine Koeppel, O.C.D. Washington, D.C.: ICS, 1993.

Stravinskas, Peter M. J. *Mary and the Fundamentalist Challenge.* Huntington, Ind.: Our Sunday Visitor, 1998.

Streep, Peg. *Mary, Queen of Heaven: Miracles, Manifestations, and Meditations on Mary.* New York: Quality, 1997.

Thérèse of Lisieux, St. *The Poetry of Saint Thérèse of Lisieux.* Trans. Donald Kinney, O.C.D. Washington, D.C.: ICS, 1996.

Wordsworth, William. *The Complete Poetical Works of William Wordsworth.* New York: T. Y. Crowell, 1907.

SELECTED BIBLIOGRAPHY

Credits continued from copyright page

"Ascension" (p. 134) from *Little Girls in Church* by Kathleen Norris, © 1995. Reprinted by permission of the University of Pittsburgh Press.

The *Sub Tuum Praesidium* (p. 135); the Salve Regina (p. 155); and the Memorare (pp. 156–7) are from the English translation of *A Book of Prayers* © 1982, International Committee on English in the Liturgy, Inc. Used with permission. All rights reserved.

The Antiphon in Honor of the Blessed Virgin (p. 160) is from the English translation of *The Liturgy of the Hours* © 1974, International Committee on English in the Liturgy, Inc. Used with permission. All rights reserved.

"Why I Love You, O Mary!" (pp. 202–5) is from *The Poetry of St. Thérèse of Lisieux*, translated by Donald Kinney, O.C.D., copyright © 1995 by the Washington Province of Discalced Carmelites, Inc., ICS Publications, 2131 Lincoln Road, N.E., Washington, D.C., 20002-1199, U.S.A. Used with permission.

MEDITATIONS ON THE LIFE OF MARY

"Heidi Hess Saxton has struck exactly the right note in her book, *With Mary in Prayer*. Always rooted in Scripture, she finds ingenious ways to reveal the humanity of Mary hidden in the spare texts. Mary is alive in this book. It is an excellent aid to meditation and prayer."

—REV. ALFRED MCBRIDE, O.PRAEM.,
professor of homiletics, Blessed John
XXIII Seminary, Weston, MA

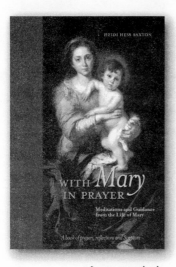

$10.95, paperback,
0-8294-1649-8

With *Mary* in Prayer

Meditations and Guidance
from the Life of Mary

Heidi Hess Saxton

With Mary in Prayer explores the events, emotions, decisions, and actions in the life of the Savior's mother. Heidi Hess Saxton has taken a deeper look at this life and has provided readers with new ways of understanding both mother and Son. Scripture quotations help to place the meditations in the context of biblical events, and the prayers allow us to connect more fully with the virtues in Mary's life that we want to develop in our own.

LOYOLAPRESS.
3441 North Ashland Avenue
Chicago, Illinois 60657

To order, call
1-800-621-1008
www.loyolapress.org